Celtic Mythology Unveiled

Exploring the Pagan Roots
of Celtic Culture.

From Ancient Beliefs
to Modern Insights.

Monica Roy

HERE IS YOU FREE GIFT!

SCAN HERE TO DOWNLOAD IT

Let's Start!

BONUS MEDITATION

EMBRACING THE FOUR ELEMENTS

Immerse yourself in Celtic wisdom through this guided meditation.

Explore the Earth, Air, Fire, and Water elements to find grounding, clarity, passion, and emotional healing.

Practice outdoors for a nature-infused connection and carry Celtic balance into your everyday life.

Table of Contents

Introduction 9

Chapter 1. The Celtic Pantheon. Gods and Goddesses of Old 11

Unveiling Celtic Deities 12

Enigmatic World of Celtic Deities 12

Deities: Nature's Weavers 13

Celtic Deities: Guardians of Spirit and Society....................................13

Divine Narratives: Celtic Gods and Goddesses....................................13

The Mighty Dagda 14

The Luminous Lug 15

The Enigmatic Morrigan..16

Cernunnos and the Horned Deities 17

The Crafty Brigit 18

Cerridwen and the Cauldron of Transformation 19

Arawn and the Realm of Annwn...20

Unearthing Celtic Origins...21

The Journey from Pre-Celtic Beliefs 21

Cultural Exchange and Celtic Deities..22

Celtic Deities' Ancestral Foundations 22

Forging the Celtic Deity Pantheon 23

Cross-Cultural Connections 24

Cernunnos: The Horned Enigma..25

Celtic Mythology and the Roman Impact 26

The Christian Influence..27

Celtic Deities: An Evolution of Spirituality 28

Chapter 2. The Mythic Landscape. Sacred Sites and Otherworldly Realms
....30

Celtic Mythic Geography: The Three Realms 31

The Celtic Cosmos..32

Realm Symbolism and Mythology 33

Nature's Impact on Land, Sea, and Sky 33

Elemental Epics: Legends of Land, Sea, and Sky................33

The Legend of the Enchanted Forest....................................33

The Legend of Lir's Children 36

Skyward Sagas: The Quest for Divine Wisdom....................37

Otherworldly Journeys: Portals, Gods, and Heroes 39

The Legend of Oisin in Tir na nÓg 41

Annwn: The Enigmatic Otherworld of Arawn 42

Mythical Landscapes: Where Reality Converges.....................45

Famous Celtic Sacred Sites and Landscapes 45

The Enchanted Oak: A Tale of the Ancestral Grove..........46

The Whispering Stones: A Tale of Standing Stones 48

Chapter 3. Tales of Heroes and Warriors. Epic Myths and Legends..........51

Legendary Heroes...52

Cú Chulainn: The Hound of Ulster.....................................53

Fionn's Quest for Wisdom 56

Unveiling Heroic Attributes and Epic Feats 58

Arthurian Legends Unveiled 59

The Legendary Chronicles of King Arthur 59

Mystical Threads in Celtic Mythology................................61

The Lady of the Lake: Keeper of Mystical Power 62

The Quest for the Holy Grail: A Spiritual Odyssey 64

The Fisher King and His Ailing Kingdom..........................64

The Pursuit of Spiritual Enlightenment.............................65

The Profound Impact of These Tales..................................66

Myths that Shaped Celtic Identity 66

Chapter 4. Goddesses and Feminine Wisdom. The Role of Women in Celtic Mythology 70

Celtic Goddesses: Deeper Insights into Feminine Divinity 71

Danu, The Earthly Mother 71

Brigid: A Goddess of Multifaceted Talents 73

Morrígan: The Enigmatic Goddess of Duality 74

Cerridwen: The Mysterious Goddess of Transformation 76

Celtic Goddesses and Nature's Bounty 79

Warrior Queens and Goddesses of Sovereignty 80

Sovereignty Goddesses: Divine Connections to Celtic Kingship 81

Profiles of Notable Warrior Queens 81

Boudicca, The Warrior Queen Who Defied an Empire 81

Medb - The Ambitious Queen of Connacht 83

How These Women Wielded Power 84

Gwenhwyfar - The Queen and Her Choices 85

Women in Celtic Society - Unveiling Their Empowerment 86

Celtic Legal Systems and Women's Rights 87

Chapter 5. Celtic Pagan Rituals and Ceremonies 89

Connecting with Nature in Celtic Rituals 89

The Ritual of the Sacred Grove 89

The Ceremony of the Four Elements 90

Druidic Ceremonies 91

Ancestor Veneration: Embracing Ancestral Wisdom 92

Divination in Celtic Paganism 95

Rites of Passage: Navigating Life's Sacred Thresholds 97

Celtic Festivals: Embracing Nature's Rhythms 100

The Dance of Nature and Spirit 100

Celtic Paganism vs. Norse Traditions 100

Samhain: Embracing the Celtic New Year 101

Beltane: Embracing Fertility and Union 102

Imbolc: The Awakening of Spring 103

Là Fhèill Brìghde: Imbolc in Gaelic Tradition 103

Yule. Winter and Rebirth of Light.. 105

Chapter 6 . The Druids Unearthed: Keepers of Celtic Secrets 108

The Druidic Path: Nature and Rituals....................................... 108

Symbolism of Celtic Rituals and Ceremonies 109

Animal Totems in Druidic Practice...................................... 111

Circles and Spirals: Symbols of Eternal Cycles............................... 113

Triskele and Triskelion: Spirals of Celtic Wisdom 114

Guardians of Sacred Sites 115

Honoring the Seasons: Druids and Celtic Festivals....................... 117

The Bardic Tradition 119

The Druidesses.. 120

Roles of Druidesses 120

Celtic Druidess Communities.. 121

Avalon: The Enigmatic Isle of Druidesses.. 121

Celtic Women: Empowerment and Integration 122

Chapter 7. Celtic Spirituality in the Modern World. A Living Tradition . 123

Neo-Paganism and Modern Celtic Pagan Paths 124

Beliefs and Rituals in the Modern Context 125

Druidry in the Modern World: Embracing Nature and Wisdom........ 126

Celtic Reconstructionism: Reviving Ancient Wisdom with Authenticity 127

Reconstructing Celtic Beliefs and Practices 128

Prominent Figures and Organizations 129

Bridging Celtic Spirituality with Wiccan Practices 129

Core Beliefs and Rituals 130

Exploring Celtic and Wiccan Traditions.. 130

Eclectic Celtic Spirituality.. 131

Celtic Spirituality in Everyday Life - A Deeper Exploration.............. 133

Simple Celtic Spirituality Practices 135

Conclusion: Nurturing the Flame of Celtic Wisdom 138

Bibliography 141

Introduction

In the heart of mist-shrouded forests, atop ancient hills, and along the rugged shores of the North Atlantic, a people whose stories and beliefs still echo through the ages thrived. Welcome to the enchanting realm of Celtic mythology, a world where gods and mortals, spirits and beasts, intertwine in a canvas of wonder and imagination.

Once upon a time, in an age long past, the Celts roamed vast territories of Europe, from the British Isles to the Iberian Peninsula, from Gaul to the edges of Asia Minor. Theirs was a culture steeped in nature's rhythms, where the turning of seasons marked the cadence of life, death, and rebirth. Through their myths, they sought to understand the mysteries of the universe, the forces that shaped their destinies, and the magic that danced in the whispering leaves of ancient oaks.

Among these pages, we embark on a journey across the ages, guided by the flickering flames of hearth and story. We'll encounter heroes like Bran the Blessed, whose wondrous adventures are entwined with destiny and fate. We'll peer into the mystical depths of Druidic wisdom, where ancient seers communed with spirits, and sacred groves held the secrets of the universe.

But this tale isn't just about the distant past. It's a story of resilience, adaptation, and the enduring power of myth. As the Celtic world encountered the tides of history, it faced challenges, shifting landscapes, and new belief systems. We'll uncover how these myths persisted, transformed, and even found new life in the modern day.

In this book, we'll delve into the pantheon of Celtic deities, from the mighty Dagda to the enigmatic Morrigan. We'll explore the realms of the Sidhe and the "Little People," whose ethereal presence still whispers in the hidden corners of the Celtic lands. We'll decipher the poetry, art, and symbols that adorned their world, giving voice to their vast cultural panorama.

And, just as importantly, we'll peer into the legacy of Celtic mythology, how it has left its indelible mark on the arts, literature, and even modern spirituality. As we traverse the misty landscapes of time, we'll uncover the threads that connect us to this ancient realm, whether through the captivating tales of King Arthur or the enchanting melodies of Celtic music.

So, dear reader, whether you're a scholar seeking to unravel the intricacies of Celtic lore or an adventurer eager to immerse yourself in the enchanting tales of old, our journey begins here. Prepare to be captivated by Celtic mythology's magic, mystery, and enduring beauty, where every page turns like a portal to a world where legends live, and the past whispers its secrets to those who listen.

Chapter 1. The Celtic Pantheon. Gods and Goddesses of Old

In the heart of mist-shrouded forests, along the rugged shores of the North Atlantic, and atop ancient hills, a pantheon of gods and goddesses thrived within the rich fabric of Celtic culture. These divine beings, often shrouded in myth and enigma, held profound significance in shaping the beliefs, values, and daily lives of the Celtic people.

Let's undertake this odyssey together. Within this exploration lies a tale deeply intertwined with my own heritage, one that reaches back to the traditions and wisdom passed down through generations, whispered by my grandfather in hushed tones as I sat at his knee by the flickering hearth.

My grandfather was a man of the land, a guardian of ancient knowledge that traversed the centuries. His eyes, weathered by time and experience, held the secrets of our Celtic heritage. It was from him that I first heard the tales of gods and goddesses, their stories woven into the very landscape that surrounded us.

As we delve into this exploration, we'll immerse ourselves in the myths and legends surrounding these divine figures. We'll seek to understand their origins, their places in Celtic cosmology, and their interactions with mortals. Through their stories, we'll gain profound insights into Celtic mythology's intricate and ever-evolving world, where gods, humans, spirits, and nature intertwine in a captivating narrative.

Prepare to step into the realm of Celtic gods and goddesses, where the lines between the earthly and the divine blur and where every legend holds a key to unraveling the Celts' culture, beliefs, and enduring mysteries. This journey is not just an academic pursuit; it's a continuation of a legacy, a story that began generations ago, around a hearth much like the one that now warms my home.

Unveiling Celtic Deities

Celtic mythology is a realm where the divine intermingles with the earthly, and at its core lies a pantheon of gods and goddesses, each holding a unique place in the hearts of the Celts. Imagine a world where gods and goddesses are not solitary figures but part of a divine ensemble, working in harmony to influence the course of nature, destiny, and human lives. This is the essence of the Celtic pantheon. In Celtic spirituality, there's no singular, all-powerful deity; instead, a collection of divine beings form a cosmic patchwork, each contributing their attributes, stories, and significance. This pantheon represents not just a collection of divine characters but a reflection of the Celts' deep connection with the world around them.

Enigmatic World of Celtic Deities

Within this pantheon, there's a complex kaleidoscope of deities, each distinct in their character, symbolism, and domain. From the mighty Dagda, known for his association with abundance and protection, to the enigmatic Morrigan, who often embodies the dual aspects of war and sovereignty, these deities are not one-dimensional figures. They reflect the multifaceted nature of the Celtic culture and the myriad experiences of human existence. We'll unravel the stories and significance of key deities, exploring their roles as protectors, creators, warriors, and guides.

Deities: Nature's Weavers

Celtic deities are deeply interwoven with the natural world. They personify the elements, sacred landscapes, and the very forces that shape the world. Their stories resonate with the rhythm of the seasons, the whispers of ancient forests, and the turbulent waters of rivers and seas.

Understanding Celtic deities means recognizing their integral connection with the environment, where they hold sway over life's cycles and mysteries. We'll journey through these natural connections, revealing how they influenced Celtic spirituality, rituals, and daily life.

Celtic Deities: Guardians of Spirit and Society

In the world of the Celts, deities were not distant, abstract beings. They were active participants in the lives of mortals, guiding, protecting, and inspiring. Beyond their roles in myths and legends, Celtic deities left an indelible mark on society and spirituality. They were invoked for blessings in times of abundance, protection in times of strife, and wisdom in times of uncertainty. We'll delve into their roles as guardians of tribes, patrons of craftsmen, and sources of inspiration for poets and bards. As we journey through their stories, we'll discover how these deities became integral to Celtic identity and continue inspiring modern-day seekers of Celtic wisdom.

Divine Narratives: Celtic Gods and Goddesses

In the core of Celtic mythology resides a pantheon of diverse deities, each with their unique myths and profound significance in Celtic culture. Let's explore these key gods and goddesses and uncover the captivating stories that defined them.

The Mighty Dagda

In the cornerstone of Celtic mythology stands a figure of colossal importance, the Mighty Dagda. He is often regarded as the father of the gods, a symbol of great wisdom and strength. But like all Celtic deities, the Dagda is not a one-dimensional character; rather, he embodies a vast weaving of attributes and myths that reflect the complexities of human existence.

At his essence, the Dagda is a god of life and death, embodying the dual nature of existence itself. He wields a massive club that can both slay and resurrect, a potent symbol of his dominion over life's ebb and flow. His cauldron, another emblematic possession, is the Cauldron of Plenty, capable of providing abundant sustenance, emphasizing his role as a generous provider.

One of the most famous tales featuring the Dagda is the story of the harp he crafted, an instrument that could control the seasons and sway the hearts of mortals and gods alike. Through this myth, we glimpse the Dagda's multifaceted nature, as a skilled artisan and a god capable of creating harmony and joy.

But Dagda's complexity extends beyond his material creations. He's a deity of desire and sensuality, often depicted as a god who embraces life's pleasures. Yet, his appetites are not solely hedonistic; they symbolize the vital force of life itself, the unending cycle of creation, and the perpetuation of the Celtic people.

Intriguingly, the Dagda also harbors a wisdom that matches his brawn. He possesses knowledge of the natural world and the cycles of time, which further deepens his connection to the Celtic people's agricultural and seasonal way of life.

To the Celts, the Dagda represented the essence of life, the necessary balance between birth and death, and the ever-turning wheel of existence. As we delve into his myths and significance, we unravel the intricate layers of this complex deity and gain insight into the heart of Celtic spirituality.

The Luminous Lug

In the pantheon of Celtic deities, Lug stands as a radiant and multifaceted god. His unique blend of talents and attributes mirrors the complexity of Celtic culture itself. Lug is often hailed as the master of many skills, and his myths reveal a god who excelled in numerous domains, from craftsmanship to music, and even as a formidable warrior. This diversity of talents made Lug a deity of immense significance to the Celts, and his influence reached into every aspect of their lives.

As a warrior, Lug was renowned for his exceptional prowess on the battlefield. He was not just a fighter but a leader of men, a charismatic figure who could rally warriors to victory. His myths are filled with tales of triumph, from his slaying of the Fomorian king Balor to his pivotal role in the Second Battle of Mag Tuired. These stories celebrated his martial might and exemplified the Celts' valor and resilience in the face of adversity.

Yet, Lug's brilliance extended far beyond the realm of warfare. He was a master craftsman, skilled in various arts and crafts. This aspect of his character reflects the Celts' deep appreciation for craftsmanship and artistic expression. Lug's myths, particularly those involving his crafting of magical weapons and tools, underscore the importance of artistry in Celtic society. They reveal a culture that held craftsmanship in high regard, where the creation of intricate and beautiful objects was not just a practical endeavor but a spiritual one.

Furthermore, Lug was a patron of music and poetry, talents that held immense cultural significance among the Celts. His connection to these artistic pursuits emphasized the role of creativity and storytelling in Celtic society. The Celts were known for their rich oral traditions, and Lug's association with music and poetry reinforced the importance of these traditions in passing down their history, beliefs, and values.

In our exploration of Lug, we'll delve into his myths and their deeper significance in Celtic culture. We'll uncover how Lug's multifaceted nature, as a warrior, craftsman, and patron of the arts, contributed to the vivid mosaic of Celtic society. His radiance not only illuminated the pages of Celtic mythology but also left an indelible mark on the culture and values of the Celtic people.

The Enigmatic Morrigan

Morrigan, the enigmatic goddess of Celtic mythology, is a figure of profound complexity. She embodies both the fierce, battle-hardened aspects of warfare and the sovereignty of the land itself. Her presence in Celtic myths is often shrouded in mystery and intrigue, as she weaves the threads of prophecies, omens, and the intricate dance between life and death. To truly understand Morrigan is to delve into the heart of Celtic spirituality and confront the multifaceted nature of existence.

On the battlefield, Morrigan is a formidable and awe-inspiring presence. She is not merely a goddess of war but a catalyst of destiny, a force that shapes the outcomes of conflicts and the fates of warriors. Her myths are often intertwined with tales of battles, where she appears as a spectral figure, foretelling doom or victory. Warriors sought her favor, believing that her blessings could turn the tide of battle in their favor. Morrigan's role in warfare speaks to the Celts' deeply spiritual connection with the concept of fate and the belief that the divine could directly influence the course of mortal lives.

Yet, Morrigan's significance goes far beyond the battlefield. She is also intimately tied to the land, representing the sovereignty and power of the natural world. In Celtic culture, the land was not merely a physical space but a living entity with its own spirit. Morrigan's connection to the land reinforces the Celts' deep reverence for nature and their belief in the interdependence of all living things. She embodies the idea that the land itself is a sacred, powerful force that shapes the destinies of its people.

Morrigan's myths are filled with symbolism and ambiguity, reflecting the complex fabric of Celtic spirituality. She defies easy categorization, often appearing as a shape-shifter who can take on various forms. This fluidity of identity mirrors the Celts' understanding of the fluid boundaries between life and death, the mortal and the divine. Morrigan challenges us to embrace the complexity of existence and recognize that life's mysteries are not always meant to be unraveled.

Cernunnos and the Horned Deities

In the heart of Celtic mythology, amidst the ancient forests and untamed wilderness, stands Cernunnos, a deity often depicted with antlers or horns. His image evokes a primal connection between the Celts and the animal kingdom, a reverence for the cycles of nature that shape their lives. Cernunnos, the guardian of the wild places, embodies the Celtic understanding that the land and its creatures are not just resources but sacred, living beings deserving respect.

Cernunnos is a symbol of the wild, the untamed, and the mysteries of the natural world. His antlers or horns, often adorned with serpents, connect him to the primal forces that govern life, death, and rebirth. When we delve into the essence of Cernunnos, we unearth the ancient Celtic belief that the wilderness is a realm where the divine intermingles with the earthly. This deity serves as a reminder that the Celts saw the sacred in grand temples, the rustling leaves of ancient oaks, and the hidden creatures of the forest.

But Cernunnos is not alone in his association with the wild and the horned. Throughout Celtic mythology, we encounter a pantheon of horned deities, each with their unique attributes and regional variations. Take, for instance, the Welsh figure Herne or the Irish god Donn. These divine beings further emphasize the profound reverence the Celts held for the wilderness. They are guardians, protectors, and symbols of the interconnectedness between humans and the natural world.

The stories and myths surrounding Cernunnos and his horned counterparts unveil a world where the boundaries between humanity and nature blur. They beckon us to contemplate the beauty and majesty of the wilderness, to recognize our place within the intricate web of life, and to acknowledge the spiritual significance of the untamed places of the earth.

As we journey deeper into the realm of Cernunnos and the horned deities, we'll uncover the rich symbolism, ancient rituals, and cultural significance that these figures held for the Celts. Their presence in Celtic mythology transcends mere folklore; it is a testament to a people whose souls were intertwined with the heartbeat of the natural world.

The Crafty Brigit

Amidst the kaleidoscope of Celtic deities, there exists a beloved figure who embodies the enduring flame of inspiration, healing, and craftsmanship. This is Brigit, a goddess whose myths illuminate the profound connection between creativity, the sacred flame, and the healing touch. As we venture into her realm, we encounter a deity whose influence reaches across a spectrum of human endeavors, from the lofty realms of poetry to the warmth of the hearth.

Brigit, often celebrated as one of Ireland's most cherished goddesses, extends her loving embrace beyond the Emerald Isle to touch the hearts of all who revere her. She is the eternal flame, a symbol of inspiration that kindles the fires of creativity in the souls of poets, bards, and artisans. As a patroness of blacksmithing, she represents the transformative power of the forge, where raw materials are shaped into tools and treasures, a reflection of the human capacity to craft both physical and metaphorical wonders.

But Brigit's grace does not end there. She is also a healer, her gentle touch capable of soothing both physical and spiritual wounds. Her presence in Celtic culture, and indeed, in the hearts of those who honor her, signifies the eternal cycle of renewal and vitality. Just as spring follows winter, Brigit reminds us that even in the darkest times, the potential for growth, healing, and the rekindling of the spirit exists.

As we delve into the myths and stories that celebrate Brigit, we'll uncover the rich mosaic of her significance in Celtic culture. Her festivals, such as Imbolc, mark the turning of seasons and the awakening of the land from its wintry slumber. Her symbols, like the perpetual flame and the sacred wells, are not mere icons but profound representations of the enduring human connection with the divine and the natural world.

Cerridwen and the Cauldron of Transformation
Within the diverse fabric of Celtic mythology, a Welsh goddess named Cerridwen stands as a guardian of profound mysteries, a weaver of transformative tales, and a keeper of the Cauldron of Transformation. Her story is a testament to the ever-turning wheel of life, where rebirth and profound change are woven into the very fabric of existence.

Cerridwen's myth is a narrative of potency, one that speaks to the depths of wisdom and poetic inspiration. At the heart of her tale lies the enigmatic cauldron, a vessel of power that bestows upon those who partake in its brew not only knowledge but the very essence of profound change. It is through this sacred vessel that the cycle of life, death, and rebirth is made tangible, a reflection of the Celtic belief in the eternal and cyclical nature of existence.

In our exploration of Cerridwen and her cauldron, we shall journey into the heart of her myth. We will witness the tumultuous narrative that unfolds as Cerridwen seeks to brew a potion of profound insight and inspiration. This potion, known as 'greal' in Welsh, holds within it the potential for personal transformation, a metamorphosis of the spirit and intellect that can elevate a mortal into a realm of divine wisdom.

As we delve deeper into this tale, we will uncover the symbolism and significance of the cauldron, a motif that echoes throughout Celtic mythology. It represents not only the transformative power of knowledge but also the crucible of life itself, where experiences, both bitter and sweet, blend to create the elixir of understanding.

Arawn and the Realm of Annwn

In the heart of Celtic mythology lies a realm of otherworldly wonder, a place where the mortal and the divine converge—the realm of Annwn, presided over by the enigmatic lord, Arawn. Within the intricate mosaic of Celtic spirituality, Arawn's realm holds a unique place, offering profound insights into the Celtic perspective on the afterlife and the mysterious dimensions beyond our mortal world.

Arawn himself stands as a guardian of this ethereal realm, a custodian of its mysteries, and a guide to those who dare to venture into its depths. His myths illuminate the journeys of mortals who have crossed the threshold between the earthly and the divine, shedding light on the significance of the Otherworld in Celtic belief.

In this exploration of Arawn and the realm of Annwn, we will delve into the stories and symbolism that define this aspect of Celtic mythology. These tales offer a glimpse into the intricate beliefs of the Celts, where death is not seen as an end but as a transition—a journey into a realm of timeless mysteries and everlasting beauty. Within these stories, we'll unearth the Celtic perspective on the afterlife, which differs from many other ancient cultures. Instead of a stark division between life and death, the Celts perceived a seamless continuum, where the mortal and the divine coexist in a harmonious dance. With Arawn as its sovereign, Annwn exemplifies this belief, offering a place of transition, transformation, and eternal wonder.

Unearthing Celtic Origins

In the closing section of this chapter, we turn our attention to the origins of Celtic deities, how they evolved from pre-Celtic beliefs, and the interactions and influences they had with other ancient cultures.

The Journey from Pre-Celtic Beliefs

The roots of Celtic mythology stretch into the depths of the past, beyond the emergence of Celtic culture itself. The Celts, a people known for their flexibility in absorbing and adapting to new influences, inherited and absorbed the beliefs of earlier cultures they encountered. These pre-Celtic beliefs, often animistic and nature-centric, laid the groundwork for the unique character of Celtic deities.

As the Celts migrated and settled across Europe, from the British Isles to continental Europe, they encountered various cultures, including the Etruscans, Greeks, and Romans. These encounters led to the syncretism of deities, where Celtic gods and goddesses sometimes merged with or adopted attributes from deities of other cultures. This cultural exchange enriched the Celtic pantheon, making it even more diverse and complex.

Cultural Exchange and Celtic Deities

The interactions between the Celts and neighboring cultures played a significant role in shaping Celtic deities. For example, the Celtic god Cernunnos, often depicted as a horned figure, exhibits similarities to the Greek god Pan and other horned deities from the ancient world. These cross-cultural influences reveal how interconnected ancient belief systems were, with gods and goddesses often transcending cultural boundaries.

Additionally, the Roman conquest of Celtic territories introduced new religious elements and deities. Some Celtic deities were equated with Roman gods and incorporated into the Roman pantheon. This complex interplay of cultures left an indelible mark on Celtic mythology, reflecting the adaptability and resilience of Celtic beliefs.

Celtic Deities' Ancestral Foundations

To truly understand the essence of Celtic deities, let's journey back to a time when beliefs were deeply rooted in the natural world. These gods and goddesses did not emerge in isolation but are closely tied to the ancient belief systems of their ancestors. Imagine a world where the boundaries between the natural and the supernatural were less distinct.

Nature's Reverence: In these ancient times, there was a profound respect for nature inherited from pre-Celtic societies. The Celts held a deep connection to the land. Celtic deities often embody this reverence for the natural world.

The Spirits in All Things: The world was seen as teeming with spirits - not just in living creatures, but in the very elements themselves. This animistic worldview underpins much of Celtic mythology, where deities were found in the rustle of leaves and the flow of rivers.

Echoes from the Ancestors: Wisdom from past generations was treasured. Ancestor worship was common, and the voices of the departed were believed to linger in the air and the earth. This respect for ancestors played a role in shaping Celtic spirituality.

Sacred Spaces: Certain places held a special significance. Hidden groves, ancient caves, and weathered stone circles were believed to be portals to the spirit world. These sites were the backdrop for rituals and are woven into the stories of Celtic deities.

Shamans and Spirit Journeys: Picture a shaman, wrapped in furs, standing beside a tranquil pool beneath the moonlight. Shamans, who could navigate between the realms, acted as intermediaries between mortals and spirits. Their practices laid the foundation for the idea of traveling between worlds in Celtic myth.

These ancient beliefs form the foundation of Celtic deities' stories. As we delve deeper into the origins of these gods and goddesses, we step into the shoes of those who lived in awe of the natural world, communed with spirits, and sought wisdom from their ancestors. This exploration helps us understand the profound link between the Celts and the spiritual world that surrounded them.

Forging the Celtic Deity Pantheon

The Celts, known for their expansive migrations, encountered neighboring cultures such as the Etruscans, Greeks, and Romans. These interactions significantly influenced Celtic mythology, leading to the synthesis of beliefs and the creation of a diverse pantheon.

Encounters with the Etruscans: The Celts' movement into the Italian peninsula brought them into contact with the Etruscans. This interaction led to the merging of deities. Celtic gods, with their characteristic horned imagery, encountered Etruscan counterparts with similar attributes. The result was the emergence of deities with hybrid qualities, reflecting a fusion of both cultures.

Echoes of Greece: As the Celts expanded, they crossed paths with the Greeks. This contact influenced Celtic deities, as some absorbed attributes from their Greek counterparts. Celtic goddesses, for instance, acquired traits reminiscent of Artemis, the Greek goddess of the hunt. This syncretism added depth and diversity to Celtic mythology.

Roman Conquests: The Roman conquests brought their pantheon into Celtic territories. The Romans often equated their gods with Celtic deities. This cultural exchange was more than just a political maneuver; it shaped the perception of Celtic gods. Celtic deities, in this context, adopted attributes of Roman gods. This blending created deities that embodied both traditions.

The synthesis of deities during these interactions introduced a remarkable complexity to the Celtic pantheon. Gods and goddesses became multifaceted figures, transcending the confines of one culture. They evolved into enigmatic beings, each layer of symbolism and attribute reflecting the interplay between different belief systems.

Cross-Cultural Connections

As we journey through Celtic mythology, we encounter fascinating instances of cross-cultural influences that enriched the pantheon of Celtic deities. Let's take a closer look at how these influences shaped and transformed some of these enigmatic figures.

Cernunnos: The Horned Enigma

Cernunnos, often depicted as a horned deity, serves as a prime example of the intricate web of cross-cultural influences within Celtic mythology. His symbolism and attributes exhibit striking similarities to the Greek god Pan and other horned deities from around the ancient world.

The Pan Connection: When we examine Cernunnos, we can't help but notice the resonance with Pan, the mischievous Greek god of the wild. Both Cernunnos and Pan are depicted with horns, embodying the untamed spirit of nature. These shared characteristics suggest a profound connection between the two deities. This cross-cultural influence demonstrates how ideas and symbolism transcended geographical boundaries, contributing to the rich pantheon of Celtic mythology.

Beyond Pan: Cernunnos' connections extend beyond Pan to include other horned deities from diverse cultures. This suggests a broader, shared archetype that resonated deeply with ancient societies. These influences didn't dilute the uniqueness of Cernunnos but, instead, added layers of complexity to his character.

Enriching Celtic Mythology: The merging of attributes from these diverse deities significantly enriched Celtic mythology. Cernunnos became a guardian of the wild, a symbol of nature's untamed beauty, and a guide to the mystical realms. His portrayal, influenced by cross-cultural encounters, highlights the dynamic nature of Celtic beliefs.

These cross-cultural connections reveal the adaptability and fluidity of Celtic mythology. Deities like Cernunnos exemplify how the Celts embraced diverse influences, weaving them seamlessly into their own belief system.

Celtic Mythology and the Roman Impact

Our exploration of Celtic mythology takes us into a period marked by profound change – the Roman conquest of Celtic territories. This pivotal moment in history introduced new religious elements and deities to Celtic culture, reshaping their mythology in remarkable ways.

The Roman Onslaught: As the Roman Empire expanded, it encountered and subjugated various Celtic tribes across Europe. This conquest had far-reaching consequences for Celtic mythology. The Romans brought with them not only military might but also their rich pantheon of gods and religious practices.

The Blending of Beliefs: The interactions between Romans and Celts led to a fascinating process known as syncretism, where deities from different cultures merged or influenced each other. This was not a one-sided affair; both Romans and Celts contributed to this exchange of beliefs.

Celtic Deities in a Roman Guise: To ease the integration of conquered Celts into the Roman Empire, some Celtic deities were equated with Roman gods and incorporated into the Roman pantheon. For instance, the Celtic goddess Epona, a deity associated with horses and fertility, was identified with the Roman goddess Venus.

Enriching the Celtic Pantheon: This syncretism had a profound impact on Celtic mythology. It added new layers of complexity to their belief system. Celtic deities took on Roman attributes and characteristics, becoming hybrid figures that reflected both Celtic and Roman influences.

A Dynamic Transformation: The Roman conquest thus catalyzed a dynamic transformation within Celtic mythology. It blurred the lines between Celtic and Roman deities, creating a fascinating interplay of cultural and religious identities.

The Enduring Legacy: While the Roman conquest marked a significant chapter in Celtic history, the legacy of this cultural exchange endures to this day. Some Celtic deities, now with Roman characteristics, continue to captivate our imagination and shape modern interpretations of these ancient figures.

The Christian Influence

While Celtic mythology and its deities continue to inspire and captivate, it's important to acknowledge the significant impact of Christianity on Celtic spirituality. The arrival of Christianity in the Celtic lands brought profound changes and transformations, including shifts in religious beliefs and practices.

Christian Syncretism: The process of Christianization in the Celtic regions often involved a degree of syncretism, where elements of Celtic deities and rituals were absorbed into Christian practices. This blending of traditions aimed to ease the transition from Celtic polytheism to Christianity and make the new faith more relatable to the Celtic people.

Saints and Celtic Deities: One notable aspect of this syncretism is the association of Celtic deities with Christian saints. Many ancient Celtic gods and goddesses were "Christianized" in this way. For instance, Brigid, a prominent Celtic goddess associated with healing and the hearth, became Saint Brigid in Christian tradition. Similarly, Lugh, a god of craftsmanship and skill, found echoes in the figure of Saint Lughaidh.

Sacred Sites: Christian churches and monasteries were often strategically built on or near ancient Celtic sacred sites, emphasizing the continuity of spirituality while redirecting devotion toward Christian figures and beliefs. This practice allowed for the preservation of some Celtic religious practices under the veneer of Christianity.

Eclipsing of Celtic Deities: Over time, as Christianity gained prominence, the worship of Celtic deities waned. Many of the stories and traditions of these ancient figures were preserved in folklore and oral traditions but took on a more mythical or folkloric character rather than being actively worshipped.

Legacy of Celtic Spirituality: The Christianization of the Celts did not erase the legacy of Celtic spirituality; rather, it transformed and adapted it to a new faith. The reverence for nature, the interconnectedness of the spiritual and natural worlds, and the cyclical view of life and death persisted in the Celtic regions, albeit with a Christian veneer.

Contemporary Exploration: In contemporary times, there is a growing interest in exploring Celtic spirituality beyond the confines of Christian syncretism. Many individuals seek to reconnect with the pre-Christian Celtic traditions, reviving ancient rituals and beliefs. This resurgence demonstrates the enduring fascination with the original Celtic deities and their cultural heritage.

Understanding the Christian influence on Celtic mythology is essential for appreciating the full spectrum of Celtic spirituality. It highlights the adaptability of Celtic beliefs and the enduring appeal of the deities, even in the face of profound religious transformation.

Celtic Deities: An Evolution of Spirituality

In tracing the origins and evolution of Celtic deities, we've embarked on a journey through the heart of Celtic mythology. We've uncovered the ancient beliefs that form the foundation of these enigmatic figures and explored how they adapted, transformed, and sometimes merged with influences from neighboring cultures.

From the animistic roots of pre-Celtic traditions to the syncretism with Greek, Roman, and Christian influences, Celtic mythology is a needlepoint of spiritual evolution. It's a testament to the Celts' openness to new ideas and their ability to assimilate and adapt while preserving the essence of their beliefs.

In our exploration, we've witnessed how Celtic deities continue to resonate with contemporary seekers. Their stories, symbols, and spirituality persist in modern culture, offering a bridge to a time when the boundaries between the mortal and divine were fluid and nature was revered as sacred.

While Christianity brought significant changes to Celtic spirituality, it did not extinguish the deep-seated reverence for the land, the cycles of life, and the interconnectedness of all things. This enduring legacy, sometimes hidden beneath the surface of Christian syncretism, is now experiencing a renaissance as individuals seek to reconnect with the ancient traditions of the Celts.

As we journey further into the realm of individual Celtic deities, we'll uncover their unique stories, attributes, and significance. We'll witness their enduring presence in the cultural fabric of humanity, reminding us that the past is not a distant echo but a living tapestry woven into the very essence of our modern world.

Chapter 2. The Mythic Landscape. Sacred Sites and Otherworldly Realms

At the essence of Celtic culture, where the mortal world and the divine intertwine, there exists a landscape suffused with enchantment and mystique.

This is not just geography; it's a realm where every hill, river, and forest breathes with the ancient stories of gods and heroes, where the boundaries between the earthly and the ethereal blur. Welcome to the mythic landscape of the Celts, where the land itself is a sacred text, and every mountain and river tells a tale.

As we venture into the mythic landscape of the Celts, we enter a world where geography transcends mere physical coordinates, becoming a profound facet of spirituality and mythology. It's a world where the contours of the land are etched with the memories of gods and goddesses, where the very earth beneath your feet has witnessed the dance of heroes and the whispers of spirits.

In this chapter, we'll explore the intricate relationship between the Celtic people and their land. We'll delve into the concept of Celtic mythic geography, a worldview that divides the world into three distinct realms: Land, Sea, and Sky. These realms are not mere geographical divisions; they are portals to a deeper understanding of the Celtic psyche, where nature is not just a backdrop but an active participant in the stories of gods and mortals.

But the Celtic mythic landscape is not limited to the mortal realm. It extends beyond the horizon into the Otherworld, a place of magic and mystery. This is a realm where gods and heroes venture on epic journeys, where the veil between life and death is thin, and where time flows differently. We'll explore how the Celts perceived the Otherworld and the means by which they accessed its secrets.

Additionally, we'll uncover the significance of sacred sites and landscapes in Celtic belief. These are places where myth and reality converge, where the divine touches the earthly, and where rituals and ceremonies have been conducted for millennia. From ancient stone circles to misty groves, these sites hold the essence of Celtic spirituality and continue to inspire awe and reverence to this day.

So, as we step into this enchanted realm of Celtic mythic landscapes, let your imagination roam freely. Picture the rolling green hills, the mysterious standing stones, and the shimmering lakes. Feel the presence of gods and heroes in the rustling leaves and the babbling brooks. In this journey, geography becomes mythology, and the land itself becomes a living testament to the enduring magic of Celtic culture.

Celtic Mythic Geography: The Three Realms

At the core of Celtic cosmology, a profound connection to the natural world thrives. The Celts viewed their universe as not a collection of disparate elements, but rather as an intricately woven fabric comprising three distinct realms: Land, Sea, and Sky. These realms weren't just geographical divisions but held deep symbolic and mythological significance.

The Celtic Cosmos

The Celts, with their keen observations of the world around them, developed a unique way of understanding the universe. To them, the cosmos was not a distant, abstract concept; it was an integral part of their daily lives. They believed that the land they walked upon, the sea that surrounded their islands, and the sky above them were not separate entities but interconnected parts of a greater whole. This holistic view of the cosmos shaped their spirituality, their mythology, and their relationship with the world.

World Division: Land, Sea, and Sky Realms

Land: The land, or 'Talamh' in Celtic, represented the earthly realm. It was the realm of mortals, where life unfolded, and where the Celts toiled and celebrated. It wasn't just a passive backdrop but an active participant in their stories. Mountains, rivers, and forests held sacred meaning and were often the settings for myths and legends.

Sea: The sea, known as 'Muire' in Celtic, was a dynamic and ever-changing realm. It symbolized the mysterious and unpredictable aspects of life. The Celts, especially those living on islands like Ireland and Britain, had a deep connection with the sea. It provided sustenance, but it also posed dangers. The Celts believed that the sea held secrets and hidden realms, much like the Otherworld.

Sky: The sky, or 'Neamh' in Celtic, was the realm of the divine. It represented the heavens, where gods and spirits resided. The Celts saw the sky as a vast, starry expanse that held both guidance and mystery. Celestial bodies, such as the sun and moon, played significant roles in Celtic mythology and the measurement of time.

Realm Symbolism and Mythology

Each of these realms was rich in symbolism and mythology. The land was seen as the realm of life and death, where the cycles of nature played out. The sea represented the liminal space between worlds, where heroes embarked on epic journeys and where the Otherworld could be glimpsed. The sky held the promise of the divine and was a source of inspiration and guidance.

Nature's Impact on Land, Sea, and Sky

The Celtic connection to these realms wasn't passive; it was active and reciprocal. The Celts believed that they were part of this cosmic weave, and their actions influenced the balance of these realms. Rituals and ceremonies were performed to honor the land and seek its fertility, to appease the sea and ensure safe voyages, and to connect with the gods in the sky.

As we delve deeper into each of these realms, we'll discover how they shaped Celtic mythology, spirituality, and daily life. We'll uncover the stories of gods and mortals who traversed these realms, leaving an indelible mark on Celtic culture. So, let us journey through the Celtic cosmos, where the boundaries between Land, Sea, and Sky are as fluid as the tales that bind them.

Elemental Epics: Legends of Land, Sea, and Sky

In Celtic mythology, the land, sea, and sky transcend their physical existence, becoming gateways to profound adventures and timeless wisdom. In this exploration, we delve into three elemental epics, each unveiling the intricate relationship between the Celtic people and their natural world.

The Legend of the Enchanted Forest

In a time long past, when the ancient oaks of the Celtic lands whispered secrets to those who would listen, there lived a hero named Bran. Bran was known far and wide for his courage, wisdom, and an insatiable curiosity that led him to the heart of the enchanted forest.

The forest, nestled between the towering mountains and the meandering river, was unlike any other in the realm. Its trees stood like ancient sentinels, their branches interwoven in a silent, majestic dance. The air was thick with magic, and the very ground seemed to pulse with life.

For generations, the Celtic people had spoken of the forest in hushed tones, for it was said to be a place where the veil between the earthly realm and the Otherworld was thin, where dreams merged with reality, and where the boundaries of time and space were fluid.

Bran had heard these tales since he was a child, sitting by the firelight as his grandmother wove stories of the forest's mysteries. As he grew, the stories called to him like a siren's song, and he knew that he must venture into the heart of the forest to uncover its secrets.

With a sturdy staff in hand and a heart full of determination, Bran set forth one crisp morning as the first rays of the sun painted the sky with hues of gold and amber. He moved deeper and deeper into the heart of the forest, guided only by the songs of birds and the whispers of the leaves.

As he journeyed further, the forest began to change. The trees grew taller and more ancient, their trunks gnarled and twisted. Strange and wondrous creatures emerged from the shadows, their eyes filled with both curiosity and caution. It was as if Bran had entered a realm untouched by time, a place where the very essence of the land itself was alive.

Days turned into weeks, and Bran faced trials and challenges that tested his resolve. He encountered mythical beasts and riddles posed by cunning spirits. Yet, he pressed on, drawn by an unseen force that seemed to guide his every step.

At last, he reached a clearing bathed in a soft, ethereal light. In the center of the clearing stood an ancient oak, its branches stretching toward the heavens like the arms of a welcoming host. Beneath the tree lay a circle of stones, weathered by centuries of wind and rain.

As Bran approached the tree, a sense of awe washed over him. He knew that he had reached the heart of the enchanted forest, a place where the earthly and spiritual realms converged. It was here that the boundaries between life and death, past and future, melted away.

Bran sat beneath the oak, his heart filled with gratitude and reverence. He felt a deep connection to the land, to the generations that had come before him, and to the mysteries of the universe. In that sacred moment, he understood that the land was not just a backdrop to life but an active participant in the grand mosaic of existence.

As the sun dipped below the horizon, Bran knew that he must leave the enchanted forest and return to the world of mortals. But he carried with him the wisdom of the land, the echoes of the past, and the promise of a deeper connection to the world around him.

Bran's journey was a testament to the Celtic belief in the profound symbolism of the land, where life and death intertwined, and where the mysteries of the universe were waiting to be uncovered. His story, like the ancient oaks of the enchanted forest, continued to whisper its secrets to those who would listen, reminding them of the timeless bond between the Celtic people and their land.

The Legend of Lir's Children

In the Celtic lands of Ireland, where emerald-green hills roll down to meet the wild, tumultuous sea, there existed a tale as old as the waves themselves. It was the story of Lir, a mighty sea god, and his four cherished children.

Lir's children were not like ordinary mortals. They possessed a beauty that seemed otherworldly, with hair like spun gold and eyes as blue as the deepest ocean. They were known far and wide for their laughter, their songs, and their deep love for the sea.

Among Lir's children, his only daughter, Fionnuala, shone the brightest. She was a creature of grace and gentleness, and her voice could rival the sweetest of birds. Fionnuala's brothers, Aodh, Fiachra, and Conn, loved her dearly and cherished the songs she sang to them.

But, as is often the way with such tales, tragedy befell this idyllic family. Lir's heart was captured by another, and he married a jealous and wicked woman named Aoife. Consumed by envy of Lir's children and their bond with the sea, Aoife's heart darkened like a storm cloud.

One fateful day, while the children were playing by the sea, Aoife cast a wicked spell upon them. She transformed them into four white swans, condemning them to spend nine hundred years upon the wild and desolate seas. They were to retain their human minds and voices but live as swans, far from the world they once knew.

As the spell took hold, the children's hearts filled with sorrow, and their laughter turned to mournful songs that echoed across the waves. Their once-golden hair turned as white as their feathers, and they soared into the sky, forever bound to the sea.

Throughout their long, solitary existence, Lir's children navigated the tempestuous seas, their wings brushing against the heavens and their voices carrying the ancient melodies of a world they had lost. They learned the secrets of the depths, the rhythms of the tides, and the mysteries of the sea.

Their tale became a symbol of the sea's beauty and its unforgiving nature, of love and loss, and of the enduring connection between the Celts and the oceans that surrounded their islands. The legend of Lir's children served as a poignant reminder that the sea, with all its majesty and danger, was an inseparable part of Celtic culture, a realm where myth and reality converged.

As the waves whispered their eternal lullaby to Lir's swan children, they carried with them the legacy of a love that had transcended the boundaries of land and sea, and the enduring enchantment of the Celtic world.

In this maritime legend, the sea was not just a backdrop but a central character, a force of both enchantment and peril. The story of Lir's children, with its themes of transformation and endurance, reflected the profound connection between the Celts and the ever-changing, unpredictable sea that shaped their lives and myths.

Skyward Sagas: The Quest for Divine Wisdom

In the heart of Celtic mythology, among the lofty peaks of the sky, where stars twinkled like ancient storytellers, there existed a longing—a yearning for celestial knowledge and enlightenment. This yearning gave rise to a series of skyward sagas, tales of heroes and seekers who embarked on cosmic journeys.

One such saga tells of a hero named Oisin, whose name meant "young deer." Oisin was a poet and warrior, a man of both wisdom and bravery. His quest for enlightenment led him to the ethereal realm of the sky, where he sought the wisdom of the ages.

Upon his celestial journey, Oisin was guided by Niamh of the Golden Hair, a fairy queen from the Otherworld. She rode upon a white steed that shimmered like the moon's glow and beckoned Oisin to follow her. Together, they soared into the boundless sky, leaving behind the earthly realm.

As Oisin ventured deeper into the celestial expanse, he encountered otherworldly beings and celestial phenomena. He witnessed the constellations come to life, their stories unfolding in the heavens above. The stars whispered ancient tales of love, valor, and destiny, revealing the interconnectedness of all things.

Oisin's quest led him to the realm of the silver apples, where wisdom flowed like a river of light. He partook of these apples, and his understanding expanded, allowing him to glimpse the mysteries of the universe. Time itself seemed to blur in this celestial realm, where past, present, and future coalesced into a single fabric of existence.

Yet, as with all sagas, Oisin's journey was not without its trials. Time passed differently in the sky, and he longed to return to the land of his birth. Niamh granted his wish, but she cautioned him not to touch the earthly soil, for doing so would bind him to the relentless passage of time.

Alas, upon his return to the earthly realm, Oisin's foot grazed the ground, and he aged in an instant, becoming a wizened old man. His once-mighty deeds and youthful vigor were but memories.

The skyward sagas of Celtic mythology were not just tales of celestial exploration; they were parables of the human quest for wisdom and enlightenment. They highlighted the sky's role as a source of inspiration and the keeper of timeless truths.

Through these sagas, the Celts sought to bridge the gap between the mortal and the divine, between the earthly and the celestial, and to understand their place in the grand fabric of existence.

In the ever-expansive sky, where stars danced in celestial choreography, the Celts found not just myths but mirrors reflecting the deepest yearnings of the human soul. These sagas, like constellations in the night sky, continue to illuminate the path to enlightenment for those who gaze upward with wonder and curiosity.

Otherworldly Journeys: Portals, Gods, and Heroes

In Celtic mythology's enchanting realm, the Otherworld concept stands as a mysterious and captivating cornerstone. This Otherworld, often referred to as 'Tír na nÓg' in Irish mythology and by various names in other Celtic traditions, represents a parallel dimension, a wondrous and perilous place where the ordinary rules of reality bend and twist. Here, mortals, gods, and heroes embarked on journeys transcending the everyday world's boundaries.

The idea of the Otherworld in Celtic mythology

The Otherworld was not a distant, unreachable place in Celtic belief; it was a realm that interpenetrated with the mortal world. It existed alongside our reality, hidden behind veils only occasionally lifted by specific events or magical means. Inhabitants of the Otherworld were seen as beings of great beauty and power, and their lands were often described as idyllic and eternal.

How mortals, gods, and heroes accessed the Otherworld

Accessing the Otherworld was not a straightforward endeavor. Mortals, gods, and heroes often required special keys or guidance to cross into this realm. These keys took various forms, including mystical portals like burial mounds or fairy hills, magical objects, or the aid of supernatural beings. For mortals, entering the Otherworld was usually an accidental or unexpected event, often occurring during quests or adventures.

Gods and heroes as intermediaries between realms

In Celtic mythology, gods and heroes frequently served as intermediaries between the mortal world and the Otherworld. They were the bridge between these realms, possessing the knowledge and power to traverse the mystical boundaries. Heroes like Cú Chulainn and Finn MacCool embarked on epic quests that led them to the Otherworld, where they encountered gods, gained wisdom, or retrieved treasures.

Heroic quests and journeys to the Otherworld

Heroic quests and journeys to the Otherworld were central motifs in Celtic mythology. They symbolized the pursuit of knowledge, spiritual growth, and the quest for treasures or wisdom. These tales showcased the bravery and resourcefulness of Celtic heroes and the importance of their connection to the divine realm. Often, the challenges and encounters faced in the Otherworld transformed heroes, granting them new insights or bestowing them with magical gifts.

As we journey through the tales of the Otherworld, we'll encounter heroes who ventured into its realms, gods who traversed the boundary between mortals and divinity, and the magical portals that connected these two worlds. These stories offer us a glimpse into the Celtic view of the cosmos, where the ordinary and extraordinary coexist, and where the line between reality and myth is often beautifully blurred.

Mortal-Divine Journeys in Celtic Mythology

In the realms of Celtic mythology, the mortal world is not bound by ordinary constraints. Mortals, gods, and heroes alike embark on extraordinary journeys, often guided by the call of the Otherworld. This section invites you to step into the shoes of these brave adventurers as they navigate the realms of gods, spirits, and elusive portals. As we explore their tales, we'll uncover the mysteries that connect the mortal and divine, and the profound significance of these journeys in Celtic belief.

The Legend of Oisin in Tir na nÓg

In the heart of ancient Ireland, where emerald hills kissed the sky and the songs of bards filled the air, there lived a hero named Oisin. He was the son of the great warrior Fionn mac Cumhaill, leader of the Fianna, a band of noble protectors.

One day, while Oisin was hunting in the forest, he encountered a scene that would change his life forever. Through the dappled sunlight and the whispering leaves of the oak trees, he saw a breathtaking sight: a beautiful maiden, radiant as the morning sun, riding a shimmering white horse. Her name was Niamh, and she was no ordinary maiden but a princess of the Sidhe, the fairy folk.

Niamh's beauty and grace struck Oisin like a lightning bolt, and he was captivated by her ethereal presence. She beckoned to him, and without hesitation, he mounted her horse and joined her on a journey like no other. They rode together, faster than the wind, through the forests, across sparkling rivers, and over emerald hills.

As they journeyed, Oisin and Niamh fell deeply in love. Time seemed to stand still in Niamh's company, and Oisin forgot the world he had known. He had entered Tir na nÓg, the Land of Youth, a realm beyond the ordinary world of mortals. In Tir na nÓg, days passed like moments, and happiness bloomed like eternal spring.

But, as all tales of enchantment go, a longing tugged at Oisin's heart. He missed his family, his friends, and the land of his birth. Niamh understood his yearning, and with a heavy heart, she allowed Oisin to return to Ireland, promising that she would join him shortly.

Oisin, filled with love and longing, mounted the white horse once more. As they crossed back into the mortal realm, he felt a strange sensation. The world around him had changed. The forests were denser, the rivers wider, and the people, clad in strange attire, stared in awe at this noble rider from a distant age.

Oisin, it turned out, had spent centuries in Tir na nÓg, and the Ireland he had known was a land of myth and legend. He sought out his former comrades, the Fianna, but found only their graves. The world he had known was gone, replaced by a new age.

In this way, Oisin's otherworldly journey was not just a matter of distance but a voyage through the mists of time itself. His love for Niamh and his experiences in Tir na nÓg had woven him into the very fabric of Celtic mythology, a living testament to the enduring allure of the Otherworld.

This legend of "Oisin in Tir na nÓg" captures the essence of otherworldly journeys in Celtic mythology, where the boundaries between the mortal realm and the mystical Otherworld blur, and where the passage of time becomes a fluid concept. It's a story of love, adventure, and the profound connections between the earthly and divine realms.

Annwn: The Enigmatic Otherworld of Arawn

In our exploration of Celtic mythology, we've encountered the concept of Otherworldly Realms, where mortals, gods, and heroes embark on extraordinary journeys that transcend the boundaries of the everyday world. These realms are places of wonder and enchantment, where the ordinary rules of reality bend and twist.

Within the intricate web of Celtic spirituality, there is a particular realm known as Annwn, ruled by the enigmatic lord Arawn. Annwn holds a unique place in Celtic belief, offering profound insights into the Celtic perspective on the afterlife and the mysterious dimensions beyond our mortal world.

Annwn, sometimes called the 'Land of the Dead' or simply the 'Otherworld' in Welsh tales, is a realm deeply associated with Arawn. Yet, it's important to understand that Annwn is just one facet of the broader concept of Otherworldly Realms within Celtic mythology.

Now, as we continue our journey, we'll unravel the tales and significance of Annwn, gaining a deeper understanding of this ethereal realm and its connection to Celtic spirituality. So, Annwn is essentially a subset of the broader concept of Otherworldly Realms in Celtic mythology, with its unique characteristics and significance.

Annwn: The Celtic Otherworld
Within the enchanting mosaic of Celtic mythology, the concept of Otherworldly Realms has long been a source of fascination. These are places where the boundaries between the mortal and the divine become porous, where the ordinary rules of reality bend and twist, and where mortals, gods, and heroes embark on journeys that transcend the boundaries of the everyday world. In this exploration, we have encountered a realm known as Annwn, a mystical and profound dimension that holds a unique place in Celtic belief, offering deep insights into their perspective on the afterlife and the mysterious dimensions beyond our mortal world.

The Celtic Perspective on the Afterlife

The Celtic perspective on the afterlife, as exemplified by Annwn and its guardian, Arawn, differs from many other ancient cultures. Instead of viewing life and death as rigidly separate states, the Celts perceived them as part of an unending cycle. This worldview embraced the idea of continuity, where death marked a transition rather than an ultimate end.

The Seamless Continuum

Annwn represented a seamless continuum where the mortal and divine coexisted. This perspective had profound implications for Celtic spirituality. It encouraged a deeper connection with the cycles of nature and the mysteries of existence. The Celts believed that every individual was part of this grand weave of life and death, and that their actions in the mortal realm influenced the balance of these forces.

Arawn's Role as Mediator

Arawn, as the guardian of Annwn, played a pivotal role in facilitating this interconnectedness. He acted as a mediator between realms, guiding souls on their journeys and ensuring the continuity of life's intricate fabric. His presence highlighted the idea that the divine was not distant but intimately involved in the human experience.

Eternal Mysteries and Everlasting Beauty

Annwn was not just a realm of transition but also a place of eternal mysteries and enduring beauty. Time flowed differently in this realm, and the laws of nature were transcended. It symbolized the Celts' profound reverence for the cycles of existence and their belief in the potential for renewal and rebirth.

As we delve deeper into the myths and significance of Annwn and Arawn, we gain a richer understanding of the Celtic perspective on life and death. It's a perspective that encourages us to embrace the cycles of existence, find meaning in the mysteries of the universe, and view death as a transformative journey into the heart of eternal wonder.

Mythical Landscapes: Where Reality Converges

In the mystical patchwork of Celtic culture, the concept of sacredness was deeply intertwined with the natural world. The Celts held a profound reverence for their environment, believing that certain places possessed an innate spiritual significance. These sacred sites, often set amidst breathtaking landscapes, became focal points for rituals, ceremonies, and myths that bridged the gap between the mortal and divine realms.

Sacredness, in the Celtic worldview, wasn't limited to places of worship but extended to the entirety of the natural world. Every hill, river, forest, and stone was imbued with meaning and significance. The Celts believed that the land itself was alive, and these sacred sites were like the beating heart of their spiritual connection with the Earth.

Famous Celtic Sacred Sites and Landscapes
Celtic lands are dotted with a multitude of sacred sites, each with its own unique mythology and significance. From the iconic Stonehenge, where the interplay of celestial bodies and Earth was celebrated, to the sacred groves dedicated to the goddess Brigit, these sites were a testament to the Celts' deep spiritual connection with their environment.

Rituals, ceremonies, and practices
Sacred sites were the stage for a myriad of rituals and ceremonies that celebrated the changing seasons, sought divine favor, or honored the ancestors. The Celts engaged in

practices such as druidic ceremonies, solstice celebrations, and offerings to appease the spirits of these places. Exploring these rituals allows us to understand the intricacies of Celtic spirituality and its deep-rooted connection to the land.

The enduring legacy of these sites

While the Celts may have faded into history, their spiritual legacy lives on. Many of these sacred sites continue to draw visitors from around the world, not only for their historical and archaeological significance but also for their spiritual resonance. Modern Celtic spirituality, often referred to as Celtic Neopaganism or Druidry, draws inspiration from these ancient practices, rekindling the connection between humanity and the natural world.

As we wander through these hallowed landscapes and explore the stories they hold, we'll come to understand how the Celts saw the sacredness in all of creation and how these sites served as bridges between the earthly and the divine, forging a deep and enduring bond between the people and the land.

The Enchanted Oak: A Tale of the Ancestral Grove

Amidst the lush, ancient forests of Celtic lands, a tale unfolds. It is the story of the Enchanted Oak, a sacred tree that stood as a sentinel to generations of Celts. This legend tells of a druidic ritual beneath its sprawling branches, where the wisdom of the ancestors was sought. The Enchanted Oak, its bark etched with countless prayers and blessings, was a living connection to the past.

A Living Sentinel: The Enchanted Oak

The Enchanted Oak, known as "Dair na Coillte" in the old tongue, was more than just a tree; it was a guardian of wisdom and a bridge to the otherworldly realms. Its gnarled branches reached towards the heavens, while its roots delved deep into the heart of the Earth. For the Celts, this oak was a symbol of endurance, much like the people it watched over.

Under the expansive canopy of the Enchanted Oak, the druids gathered. Cloaked in robes of green and brown, they moved with deliberate grace, their eyes carrying the weight of ages. The Enchanted Oak was their sanctum, the place where they communed with the spirits of the land and the ancestors who dwelled in the Otherworld.

Whispers of the Ancients
As the sun dipped below the horizon and the forest was cloaked in shadows, the druids kindled a sacred fire. Its warm glow danced upon their faces, illuminating the reverence in their eyes. In the heart of this ancient grove, they began to chant. Their voices, a melodic hymn, resonated with the rustling leaves and the sigh of the wind through the branches.

The chant, passed down through generations, was a key to the door of the Otherworld. It was said that as the druids sang, the veil between the realms grew thin. The Enchanted Oak, a witness to countless rituals, seemed to come alive. Its leaves rustled in response, as if acknowledging the presence of the spirits.

The Ancestral Wisdom
In the heart of this mystical narrative, the druids unveiled the rituals and practices that defined these sacred groves. They made offerings of fruits, symbolizing the bounties of the Earth, and flowers, representing the beauty of life. With each chant and each offering, the connection between the living and the ancestral spirits grew stronger.

The Enchanted Oak, with its roots firmly grounded in the past, was a living testament to the enduring bond between the Celts and their sacred landscapes. It held the wisdom of the ages within its gnarled bark, whispered secrets from long-forgotten times, and cradled the hopes and dreams of generations yet unborn.

As we walk this path of the druids, we glimpse into a world where the mundane and the mystical intertwine. The Enchanted Oak and its sacred grove remind us of the profound connection the Celts had with their environment, where every tree, stone, and river held the echoes of ancestral voices. This enchanting tale invites us to explore the living history of Celtic spirituality and the enduring magic of the natural world.

The Whispering Stones: A Tale of Standing Stones

In the rolling hills of ancient Celtic lands, another legend unfolds, whispered by the standing stones that have witnessed centuries of human existence. This tale centers around a particular circle of standing stones, known as the Whispering Stones, and the mystical ceremonies that took place within their sacred embrace.

The Guardians of Time

The Whispering Stones, or "Cloch a' Bhruidhinn" as they were called in the ancient tongue, were unlike any other stones. They stood tall and proud, arranged in a perfect circle as if guarding a hidden secret. To the Celts, they represented a passage through time itself. Each stone was believed to hold the memories and wisdom of countless generations.

Under the open sky, as the sun dipped below the horizon, the druids and the Celtic community would gather around the Whispering Stones. These gatherings were not mere ceremonies but a communion with the ages. The stones were thought to act as conduits, connecting the living with the ancestors who had long departed this world.

Voices from the Past

As the stars began to shimmer overhead, a sense of reverence filled the air. The druids, adorned in their sacred robes, would begin to chant ancient verses that resonated with the very stones beneath their feet. These chants were the key to unlocking the memories held within the stones.

As the druids chanted, the stones seemed to awaken. They vibrated with an almost ethereal energy, and whispers of long-forgotten tales filled the night. It was as if the voices of the past were being channeled through these timeless sentinels. The stories they told were of heroes, of love, and of the struggles and triumphs of generations past.

A Passage Through Time

The Whispering Stones were not just storytellers; they were a bridge to the past. During these ceremonies, it was said that those in attendance could catch glimpses of their own ancestors. They would see their faces in the flickering torchlight and hear their voices in the ancient tales.

These gatherings were a reminder that the past was not lost but an integral part of the present. The stones held the collective memory of the Celtic people, connecting the living with their forebears. In this way, the Celts sought guidance, wisdom, and a profound sense of belonging.

The Living Legacy

As we step into the realm of the Whispering Stones, we uncover not only a legend but a profound practice that highlighted the Celts' deep reverence for their ancestors and the interconnectedness of all generations. The stones' whispers reveal the enduring legacy of the Celtic people and their belief that the past, present, and future are threads woven into the same fabric of existence.

This enchanting tale invites us to explore the timeless bond between the Celts and the stones that stood as silent witnesses to the passage of time. It is a testament to the enduring magic of these sacred landscapes and the profound connection the Celts maintained with their ancestral spirits through the stones' whispers.

As we wander amidst these hallowed stones and explore the stories they hold, we come to understand the rich vast mosaic of Celtic spirituality, where the voices of the past echo in the present, and where the living and the ancestors are forever intertwined.

Chapter 3. Tales of Heroes and Warriors. Epic Myths and Legends

Deep within Celtic mythology, where gods and humans come together in a complex interplay of destiny, another group of individuals takes the spotlight: the legendary heroes and warriors. These towering figures, immortalized in epic tales, are the embodiment of valor, wit, and indomitable spirit. They stand as guardians of their people, champions of justice, and icons of resilience. As we step into this chapter, we find ourselves amidst a realm where heroism knows no bounds, where battles are fought with courage, and where epic adventures await those willing to tread the path of legends.

Throughout the ages, these tales of heroes and their extraordinary exploits have resonated with cultures far beyond the Celtic lands. Heroes like Cú Chulainn, Fionn mac Cumhaill, and others have inspired countless generations with their feats of strength, wisdom, and daring. Their stories continue to echo through the corridors of time, reminding us of the timeless themes that unite humanity—valor, sacrifice, and the enduring quest for truth.

In this chapter, we journey through the vibrant kaleidoscope of Celtic hero myths, each thread woven with the essence of a hero's character and the lessons they impart. From the swashbuckling adventures of Fionn mac Cumhaill to the tragic heroics of Cú Chulainn, we'll explore these legendary figures in detail, unveiling the qualities that make them iconic. As we delve into their stories, we'll not only unravel their exploits but also uncover the cultural memory these myths preserve—the unique identity, values, and aspirations of the Celtic people.

But heroism in Celtic mythology is not confined to the deeds of a few exceptional individuals. It extends to the very essence of Celtic identity, shaping their collective memory and inspiring future generations. Beyond the battles and adventures, we'll delve into how these myths have been handed down through the ages, becoming a mirror to the Celtic soul and a source of inspiration for modern storytelling.

So, dear reader, prepare to embark on a heroic journey through the annals of Celtic mythology, where courage knows no bounds, and where the tales of these legendary figures continue to ignite the spark of heroism in us all.

Legendary Heroes

In the mosaic of Celtic mythology, legendary heroes stand as vibrant threads woven through the rich fabric of tales and legends. These heroes, often endowed with extraordinary abilities and boundless courage, are the embodiment of Celtic ideals and aspirations. Through their remarkable feats, they illuminate the path of honor, valor, and resilience for generations to come.

Exploring the Legends of Heroes
In the intricate fabric of Celtic mythology, the stories of legendary heroes shine as brilliant threads. These heroes, marked by their exceptional qualities and boundless valor, epitomize the very essence of Celtic ideals. Their tales are a testament to the indomitable human spirit, a beacon of courage, and a wellspring of cultural wisdom.

Cú Chulainn: The Hound of Ulster

Deep within the ancient realm of Ulster, where legends spring to life and destinies take their shape, the name Cú Chulainn reverberates like a resounding thunderclap. His epic tale, a symphony of trials and adventures, is a masterpiece of heroism, woven with threads of unparalleled bravery and indomitable will.

Cú Chulainn's journey commenced not as a hound of war, but as a young boy named Sétanta. Yet, fate had other designs for him. One momentous day, as he ventured towards the home of Culann the smith, he came face to face with a fierce guard dog. Without hesitation, Sétanta confronted the snarling beast, and in the battle that followed, he unintentionally slew the hound. Such an act could have incited great anger, but Sétanta was no ordinary lad; his destiny was one of greatness.

In response to his inadvertent transgression, Sétanta took an oath before Culann. He vowed to make amends by protecting and nurturing a new guard dog until it reached maturity. While the new guard dog was not yet fully grown at the time of the oath, it was indeed present in the house of Culann. This new dog symbolized Sétanta's commitment to care for and safeguard it. As such, he earned the name "Cú Chulainn," signifying "Culann's Hound."

This oath and act of making amends marked a pivotal moment in Sétanta's journey and his transformation into the legendary hero known as Cú Chulainn. It was through this commitment that the transition from the boy to the hero took root, and Cú Chulainn's legacy as Culann's Hound began.As the years passed, Cú Chulainn's renown as a warrior grew, and he became a beacon of hope for the people of Ulster. His defining moment came with the theft of a prized brown bull, an act that would plunge Ulster into a dire predicament. Queen Medb of Connacht, driven by greed and ambition, coveted this bull, and her armies marched upon Ulster with an insatiable desire to claim it.

However, the men of Ulster were cursed and incapacitated, left in a state of agony and helplessness. Only Cú Chulainn, due to a quirk of fate, remained untouched by the curse. Undaunted and resolute, he stood as the last line of defense against the approaching Connacht forces.

With superhuman strength and unrivaled combat skills, Cú Chulainn challenged the armies of Connacht. Day after day, he faced wave upon wave of adversaries, leaving a trail of foes in his wake. His name struck fear into the hearts of the Connacht warriors, yet they pressed on, driven by their queen's insatiable desire.

Cú Chulainn's defense of Ulster was not merely a display of physical prowess; it was a testament to his unwavering determination and indomitable spirit. He embodied the very essence of heroism, standing firm in the face of overwhelming odds, defending his homeland with a fiery passion that could not be quenched.

But Cú Chulainn's heroism extended beyond the battlefield. It was his loyalty and sense of honor that truly set him apart. One of the most poignant chapters in his saga revolves around his unwavering commitment to his friend and foster-brother, Ferdiad. Fate, cruel and unrelenting, pitted them against each other in a tragic duel.

Despite the inevitability of their clash, Cú Chulainn and Ferdiad faced each other with heavy hearts. They battled not out of malice, but out of duty and honor. Their duel, while heart-wrenching, showcased the depth of Cú Chulainn's character and his unyielding adherence to the warrior's code.

As we journey through the epic narratives of Celtic mythology, the story of Cú Chulainn stands as a testament to the enduring power of heroism, where valor, loyalty, and honor converge in the crucible of destiny. His legend continues to inspire, reminding us that heroism isn't merely a feat of physical strength but a reflection of the noblest aspects of the human spirit.

Cú Chulainn's Attributes and Feats

At the center of Cú Chulainn's heroism lay a range of exceptional attributes. His battle frenzy, known as the "ríastrad," transformed him into an unstoppable force, with eyes like fiery embers and muscles bulging with superhuman strength. This berserk state allowed him to perform incredible feats on the battlefield, defeating numerous opponents single-handedly.

He also possessed the "gae bolga," a deadly spear with barbed heads that could only be removed by the person who inflicted the wound. This weapon struck with pinpoint accuracy and was nearly impossible to defend against, adding to Cú Chulainn's fearsome reputation.

Despite his fierce combat abilities, Cú Chulainn had a tender side. He harbored deep love for Emer, whom he pursued through a series of trials to win as his wife. His commitment to their love stands as a testament to his romantic nature amidst the chaos of battle.

Lessons in Heroism and Culture

Cú Chulainn's story transcends mere legend; it carries profound moral and cultural lessons. His loyalty, sense of duty, and honor exemplify the core values of Celtic heroism. In his unwavering defense of Ulster, we see the Celtic commitment to protecting one's homeland and people at all costs.

His tale also reflects the intricate relationship between the individual and their community, a vital aspect of Celtic culture.

Cú Chulainn's actions, even in the midst of his frenzied battles, were driven by a sense of responsibility to those he cared for.

Cú Chulainn's heroism continues to inspire to this day. His legend reminds us that true heroism extends beyond physical prowess; it encompasses virtues such as honor, loyalty, and selflessness. In the ever-turning wheel of Celtic mythology, Cú Chulainn's name remains etched as a beacon of heroism and honor, an enduring symbol of the Celtic spirit.

Fionn's Quest for Wisdom

Fionn mac Cumhaill, often simply referred to as Fionn, emerges from the annals of Celtic mythology as a beacon of wisdom and sagacity. While his contemporaries might have been renowned for their physical prowess, Fionn's true strength lay in his keen intellect and ability to navigate the intricate landscapes of the mind.

Fionn's journey into the realm of wisdom centers around a sacred creature, the Salmon of Knowledge. This enigmatic being, caught in the River Boyne, held the sum of all knowledge in its flesh. It was said that whoever consumed this salmon would gain unparalleled insight into the mysteries of the world.

Guided by the wisdom of his druidic mentor, Finnegas, Fionn undertook the quest to capture and cook the Salmon of Knowledge. This endeavor was not one of sheer might but required patience, cunning, and precision. When the time came, and the salmon was cooked to perfection, Fionn inadvertently burnt his thumb on the sizzling flesh and instinctively placed it in his mouth to soothe the pain.

In that moment, the wisdom contained within the salmon's flesh surged into Fionn. From then on, he possessed the knowledge and insight of ages past, granting him a unique perspective and a reputation as one of the wisest beings in Celtic mythology.

Fionn's Wisdom in Action

Fionn's wisdom was not a passive gift but a tool he employed to benefit his people. His quick wit and clever stratagems were pivotal in resolving disputes, navigating treacherous situations, and outsmarting adversaries. While others relied on physical might, Fionn's wisdom allowed him to triumph through intellect and guile.

One of his most famous tales involves the 'Salmon Leap,' a poetic competition that showcased not only Fionn's wisdom but also his profound connection to nature. The competition required participants to compose verses while perched on one leg, amidst the tumultuous waters of the River Boyne. Fionn, drawing inspiration from the very river that had gifted him wisdom, excelled in this test of both mind and body.

Fionn's Legacy

Fionn's story serves as a reminder that heroism can manifest in diverse ways. While Cú Chulainn's heroism was marked by ferocity and strength, Fionn's was characterized by wisdom, diplomacy, and a profound understanding of the world.

In Celtic culture, where storytelling and poetic inspiration held immense significance, Fionn's legacy endures as a symbol of the power of knowledge and intellect. His tales emphasize that true heroism encompasses not only physical valor but also the ability to navigate the complexities of life with wisdom and insight. In the vast pantheon of Celtic mythology, Fionn mac Cumhaill's name stands as a testament to the multifaceted nature of heroism and the enduring value of wisdom.

Unveiling Heroic Attributes and Epic Feats

Celtic heroes are not mere warriors; they embody a set of virtues that define their heroism. Courage, loyalty, honor, and a deep connection to the land are the hallmarks of these legendary figures. They stand as protectors of their people and defenders of the natural world. Their exploits, whether in the heat of battle or the pursuit of knowledge, are tales of inspiration and heroism that continue to resonate with modern audiences.

Mythical Hero Stories and Moral Lessons

Beyond their larger-than-life adventures, the stories of Celtic heroes carry profound moral and cultural lessons. They teach us the value of bravery in the face of adversity, the importance of honor and loyalty, and the enduring connection between the Celts and their land. These myths serve as mirrors, reflecting the core values and aspirations of Celtic society. They remind us that heroism isn't confined to the realms of gods and legends but is a path that mortals can tread, leaving a lasting legacy for all to admire.

Epic Battles and Adventures

In the heart of Celtic mythology lies a treasure trove of epic battles and daring adventures. These tales, often passed down through generations via oral tradition before being recorded in manuscripts, are the crucible of heroism, honor, and the relentless pursuit of glory.

Celtic mythology isn't just a pantheon of gods and heroes; it's a rich mosaic of struggles and conquests, where champions rise to meet insurmountable challenges. These stories transport us to a time when warriors, often bolstered by mystical artifacts and guided by prophecies, faced off against formidable foes. They carry us across landscapes both real and mythical, from the verdant plains of Ireland to the misty hills of Arthurian legends.

These epic battles and adventures aren't just stories of valor; they are the very essence of Celtic identity. They echo the fierce independence, courage, and deep-rooted connection to the land that defined Celtic culture. As we immerse ourselves in these tales, we'll unravel their cultural and historical significance and discover how they continue to shape Celtic art, literature, and the enduring sense of identity among the Celtic people. So, buckle your metaphorical armor and prepare to embark on these thrilling journeys that have enthralled generations and will continue to do so for ages to come.

Arthurian Legends Unveiled

Within the annals of Celtic mythology, two sets of epic narratives stand as towering giants: the Táin Bó Cúailnge and the Arthurian legends. These sagas, while originating from different corners of the Celtic world, share an indomitable spirit of heroism, chivalry, and the pursuit of a noble ideal.

The Legendary Chronicles of King Arthur

Among the mosaic of Celtic mythology, Arthurian legends stand as a testament to the enduring allure of heroic narratives. These legends, primarily associated with the legendary King Arthur, have captured the imaginations of countless generations.

At the heart of the Arthurian legends is the figure of Arthur himself, a hero-king whose story traverses the realms of history and mythology. While Arthur's existence as a historical figure is still debated, his mythical persona is firmly rooted in Celtic lore.

The Arthurian legends, often set against the backdrop of a mythical Britain, tell the tale of a king destined to unite a fractured land and establish a golden age of chivalry and honor. Central to these tales is Arthur's iconic sword, Excalibur, and the enigmatic Lady of the Lake, who bestows this legendary weapon upon him.

One of the most famous elements of the Arthurian cycle is the Knights of the Round Table, a fellowship of noble knights who exemplify chivalry and honor. Led by Arthur, these knights embark on epic quests, the most famous of which is the quest for the Holy Grail, a vessel with miraculous powers.

The character of Merlin, a wise and enigmatic sorcerer, adds a layer of mysticism to the legends. Merlin's prophetic abilities and counsel guide Arthur in his quest to establish a just and unified kingdom.

The Arthurian legends are not merely tales of valor and quests but also narratives that explore the complexities of human nature. They delve into themes of betrayal, love, and the pursuit of an idealized code of conduct. The doomed love affair between Lancelot and Guinevere, Arthur's queen, and the tragic fate of Mordred, Arthur's son and nemesis, add depth and nuance to these legends.

The enduring appeal of Arthurian legends lies not only in the grandeur of the quests and battles but also in the moral and ethical dilemmas faced by its characters. The legends resonate with themes of honor, loyalty, and the eternal quest for a more just and noble world.

These tales have left an indelible mark on Western literature and culture. They have inspired numerous adaptations, from medieval romances to modern novels, films, and television series. The search for the historical Arthur may continue, but the mythic Arthur, the legendary king who sought to create a better world, lives on in the hearts and minds of those who continue to be captivated by his timeless story.

The Arthurian legends remind us of the enduring power of myth and the profound impact of heroic narratives on our collective imagination. They embody the timeless values of courage, honor, and the pursuit of noble ideals, offering us a glimpse into the heroic spirit that has been a part of human culture for millennia.

Mystical Threads in Celtic Mythology

Within the intricate web of Arthurian legends, intertwined with elements of chivalry, medieval romance, and heroic quests, there are threads that trace back to the ancient beliefs and tales of Celtic mythology. These legends, which have captivated the imaginations of generations, are more than mere tales of valor and honor. They are, in many ways, an intricate reflection of the spiritual and cultural mosaic woven by the Celtic people.

The Celts, who once roamed the lands of Britain and Ireland, held a profound reverence for the natural world. They saw the divine not only in grand temples or holy scriptures but also in the rustling of leaves, the babbling of brooks, and the whispering winds. Their myths and traditions were intimately intertwined with the rhythms of the earth, the seasons, and the mysteries of the cosmos.

Within this section, we embark on a journey to explore two tales that resonate with Celtic spirituality and paganism, shedding light on their enduring significance. These stories serve as bridges between the world of King Arthur's Camelot and the ancient Celtic realms, offering glimpses of a shared cultural and spiritual heritage.

Through these narratives, we shall uncover how the Arthurian legends, despite their medieval European setting, resonate with the spiritual essence of the Celts, and how they continue to captivate our hearts and minds today. As we delve into these stories, let us be guided by the ancient wisdom that saw divinity not only in grand cathedrals but also in the rustling of leaves and the depths of the mystical waters.

The Lady of the Lake: Keeper of Mystical Power

In the age when Arthurian legends held sway over the hearts and minds of those who longed for the glint of a knight's armor and the promise of chivalrous quests, there existed a character both mysterious and potent—the Lady of the Lake. Within her story, we uncover echoes of ancient Celtic reverence for nature and its spiritual significance, as well as an enigmatic figure whose name, Nimue, Viviane, or Niniane, whispered through the legends.

Birth of Legends

The very birth of the Lady of the Lake is wrapped in myth and fable. Some say she was once a mortal, her path forever altered by magic, while others insist she was a being born of the ancient Celtic deities themselves. In one telling, she is the offspring of none other than the formidable sorceress, Morgan le Fay, a name resonating with its own legend.

And then there's the name—"Lady of the Lake." It's a name that drifts like mist above the waters, signifying her bond with a mystical body of water that cradles her, Avalon's embrace. Within its depths, the line between the mundane and the ethereal is gossamer-thin, making it a place where reality and myth intertwine.

The Sword of Sovereignty

At the heart of Arthurian legend lies a pivotal moment where the Lady of the Lake and King Arthur intersect, their fates forever intertwined. The Lady emerges from the tranquil waters, her presence as ethereal as the dawn's first light. In her outstretched hand, she cradles Excalibur—a blade bathed not just in the brilliance of its steel, but in the radiance of destiny itself.

Legend has it that Arthur, facing dire straits with his initial sword shattered in the crucible of battle, meets the Lady in this pivotal hour. Her arm, like an apparition, ascends from the depths of Avalon's mystical lake, Excalibur's blade gleaming as if forged by the very gods of old. With a grace that defies the mortal realm, she offers him this legendary weapon, sealing Arthur's fate as Britain's rightful sovereign.

The Keeper of the Sword's Return
Yet, the Lady's connection to Arthur doesn't culminate with the bestowal of the sword. In the hauntingly poetic finale of Arthur's saga, as the wounded king returns to the sacred waters, it is once again to the Lady of the Lake that he turns. Excalibur, symbolizing not just sovereignty but the very essence of his reign, is returned to its watery home. Only she, with her profound mystical connection, can safely cradle the sword, guarding it until the day Arthur is prophesied to return.

The Enigmatic Guardian
Excalibur is not the sole treasure under the Lady's guardianship. In certain iterations of the legend, she serves as the protector of the sword's scabbard, a mystical relic said to render its wearer impervious to mortal harm. These treasures position her as the protector of ancient wisdom, a keeper of the sacred, her spirit deeply entwined within the very essence of Arthurian legend.

A Bridge Between Worlds
Yet, the Lady of the Lake's allure goes beyond her role as a guardian of mystical relics. She personifies a profound connection to the Otherworld, symbolized by the mystical lake she calls home. She is the ethereal bridge linking not only the ordinary and the magical but also the realms of the divine and

the human. Her character embodies the age-old Celtic belief in the interconnectedness of all existence, where the natural world itself is a canvas woven with threads of the divine.

With the Lady of the Lake as our guide, we embark upon an odyssey into the mystical heart of Arthurian legend. Her story beckons us to traverse the concealed depths of her mythology and the resonant chords of Celtic spirituality that thrum within it—a sojourn through the veils of time and enchantment.

The Quest for the Holy Grail: A Spiritual Odyssey

The Arthurian legends spiral into the realm of the mystic once more, this time with the enigmatic Holy Grail at their center. The Holy Grail, a vessel of boundless power and spiritual significance, beckons knights on a quest unparalleled in its divine aspirations. And at the heart of this quest lies yet another connection to the ethereal—the enigmatic Fisher King and the guiding hand of the Lady of the Lake.

The tale commences when King Arthur's knights, chosen for their valor and purity of heart, embark on a sacred mission: the Quest for the Holy Grail. This quest isn't just a physical journey but a profound spiritual odyssey. It's a pursuit of the divine, an exploration of the deepest reaches of the soul, where earthly and spiritual realms converge.

The Fisher King and His Ailing Kingdom

Central to the Grail quest narrative is the Fisher King, also known as the Maimed King. His kingdom languishes in perpetual desolation, mirroring his own grievous wound. The fate of the land and its ruler are inextricably linked; as he suffers, so does his realm.

Yet, within this melancholic narrative, the promise of redemption emerges—a glimmer of hope manifested through the Holy Grail. This sacred vessel possesses the power to heal the Fisher King's wound and, by extension, restore vitality to his ailing kingdom.

As with many elements of Arthurian legend, the Lady of the Lake casts her presence upon this spiritual odyssey. She emerges as a spiritual guide, a guardian of profound wisdom, and a keeper of the Grail's secrets. It's she who appears to Sir Percival, one of the Grail quest's knights, offering insight and counsel that transcends the boundaries of the ordinary world.

The Pursuit of Spiritual Enlightenment

The Quest for the Holy Grail becomes a test not just of valor but of spiritual purity and enlightenment. Knights must navigate treacherous terrain, facing moral dilemmas and spiritual trials. The Grail often appears elusive, shimmering at the edges of their perception, calling them deeper into the mystical folds of their existence.

This epic quest is more than a simple adventure; it's a spiritual exploration of the deepest questions of human existence. The knights' journey reveals themes of redemption, healing, spiritual enlightenment, and the interconnectedness of the material and spiritual realms.

As the story unfolds, we find ourselves not merely traversing the realms of medieval chivalry but diving into the profound waters of spirituality. With the Lady of the Lake as our guide and the Quest for the Holy Grail as our vessel, we set forth into the heart of Arthurian mysticism, where the boundaries between the earthly and the divine blur, and the human spirit soars towards enlightenment.

The Profound Impact of These Tales

These epic narratives carry profound cultural and historical significance, offering insights into Celtic societies.

Culturally, they serve as mirrors reflecting Celtic values, such as courage, loyalty, and a deep connection to the land. The heroes embody these cherished virtues, instilling a sense of identity and shared values among the people.

Historically, the stories offer glimpses into the tumultuous times they emerged from, echoing actual events and power struggles. For instance, Arthurian legends parallel the post-Roman era in Britain.

Furthermore, these tales have left an indelible mark on Celtic literature, art, and politics. They continue to inspire contemporary works, highlighting their lasting impact on Western culture.

Myths that Shaped Celtic Identity

In the heart of every culture, beneath the layers of history and time, lies a treasure trove of stories. These aren't just tales spun for amusement; they are the threads that weave the very fabric of a people's identity. Among the Celts, this treasure was found in myths and legends - stories of heroes, gods, and the land itself.

Stories Carved in the Celtic Soul. In a Windswept Celtic Hill

Imagine standing on a windswept Celtic hill, surrounded by the whispers of the past. Here, myths weren't just fanciful narratives; they were a living, breathing repository of a culture's collective memory. They held within them the echoes of battles fought, the wisdom of ancestors, and the values that bound the community together.

Cultural memory, as expressed through myths, was a way for the Celts to remember their origins, their triumphs, and their shared identity. These stories served as a mirror reflecting the values they held dear - bravery, honor, loyalty, and an unbreakable bond with the land.

Myths were more than just tales told around the fire; they were the foundation upon which Celtic communities were built. They weren't static relics of the past but living narratives that adapted and evolved, just as the culture did. They offered guidance and inspiration to each new generation, passing down the essence of Celtic identity.

Keepers of Ancient Tales. The Legacy of Storytellers
In the heart of Celtic communities, there existed a revered class of individuals known as storytellers. They were the keepers of ancient tales, the torchbearers of Celtic culture's vast canvas of myths and legends. These storytellers, often called seanchaí in Ireland, held a sacred duty - to ensure that the heroic traditions and values of their people endured.

Gathered around hearths, in the flickering light of torches, or beneath the vast expanse of starry skies, these storytellers wove tales of heroism and wonder. Their words resonated with a poetic cadence, infusing life into ancient narratives. Through their storytelling prowess, the myths of Cú Chulainn's valor and Fionn mac Cumhaill's wisdom lived on, not as mere stories of the past, but as living, breathing parts of Celtic culture.

Oral Epics: The Poetry of Heroes. Words Carved in Memory
Before the written word became prevalent, Celtic hero myths were preserved through the power of oratory. Bards, druids, and skilled storytellers were the torchbearers of this oral tradition. They recited these tales with precision and eloquence, captivating audiences with every word.

The form of these oral epics was not arbitrary; it was a deliberate choice. The poetic cadence, meter, and rhyme schemes were designed not only to captivate listeners but also to aid in memorization. Every line, every verse, was a thread in the intricate tapestry of Celtic identity, ensuring that these sagas were faithfully passed down through the generations.

The Enduring Magic of Repetition. Echoes Across Generations

Storytellers understood the power of repetition in embedding these narratives in the cultural psyche. Celtic myths often followed episodic structures, where key events and moral lessons were revisited. This repetition wasn't redundant; it was a deliberate tool to reinforce important values and the ideals of heroism.

By hearing these stories repeatedly, each generation internalized the values and virtues extolled in the myths. The courage of Cú Chulainn, the loyalty of the Knights of the Round Table, and the wisdom of Fionn mac Cumhaill became more than distant tales; they became guiding principles for life.

A Living Connection. Bridging Generations

Through storytelling, Celtic communities created a living connection with their past. The heroes of these sagas were not distant figures but revered ancestors. This sense of kinship with the heroic past fostered a deep-rooted pride in one's cultural identity.

Imagine a young Celt, wide-eyed with wonder, listening to the stories of their ancestors. These narratives weren't just adventures; they were a blueprint for living. They provided a moral compass, a guide on how to navigate life's challenges with honor and integrity.

Continuity in the Modern World. Storytelling's Modern Renaissance

Today, while the tradition of oral storytelling has given way to the written word and digital media, the power of storytelling endures. Hero myths continue to inspire and educate. They bridge the gap between the ancient Celts and contemporary audiences, ensuring that the heroic traditions remain alive and relevant.

From books to theater to digital platforms, hero myths find new life. They serve as a reminder of the universal struggles and triumphs that connect generations. They're a testament to the enduring nature of the human spirit, reminding us that, like the heroes of old, we too can overcome adversity with courage and resilience.

The Torch Passed On

In the end, the role of storytelling in passing down heroic traditions through generations is a testament to the enduring power of narrative in shaping culture and identity. These tales, once spoken around campfires and in grand halls, continue to illuminate our path, reminding us of the timeless values and virtues that define the essence of heroism. Through storytelling, we become the custodians of our shared heritage, entrusted with the responsibility of preserving and celebrating the heroic traditions that bind us to our roots.

Chapter 4. Goddesses and Feminine Wisdom. The Role of Women in Celtic Mythology

Within Celtic mythology, where legends of heroes and epic battles reside, there exists another equally captivating realm— a realm of feminine wisdom, divine grace, and formidable strength. In this chapter, we explore the intricate fabric of Celtic culture, where women played pivotal roles in shaping the myths and society of the Celts.

Imagine standing on the misty shores of ancient Ireland or the rugged landscapes of Scotland. The air is charged with an inexplicable energy, a whisper of something timeless and profound. Here, the Celts held a deep reverence for both the tangible and the mystical, and this reverence extended to the feminine. To understand the role of women in Celtic mythology, we must first embrace the essence of this culture—an essence entwined with nature's rhythms, where goddesses and earthly women alike were revered.

As we journey deeper into Celtic mythology, we'll unravel the stories of Celtic goddesses—powerful, enigmatic beings who personified the natural world and its mysteries. These goddesses were not distant or aloof figures but intimate parts of daily life. They embodied the cycles of fertility, the magic of transformation, and the wisdom of the land.

But our exploration doesn't end with goddesses alone. We'll also meet warrior queens, leaders of their people, and the embodiment of sovereignty. These remarkable women weren't bound by the limitations of their time; they were pioneers of empowerment, wielding influence and authority in a society that valued their contributions.

In this chapter, we'll delve into the world of Celtic goddesses, warrior queens, and the women who shaped Celtic society. We'll uncover the multifaceted roles they played, from guardians of nature's secrets to queens who governed with grace and strength. Together, we'll unveil the profound impact of women in Celtic culture and how their legacy endures as a source of inspiration and empowerment. So, let us step into this mystical realm, where the feminine is celebrated, and the stories of women in Celtic mythology come to life.

Celtic Goddesses: Deeper Insights into Feminine Divinity

In the verdant landscapes of Celtic mythology, where ancient forests whispered secrets and rivers sang songs of the past, the presence of goddesses was as palpable as the earth beneath one's feet. These were not distant deities but living, breathing embodiments of the land itself.

Imagine a pantheon where nature's forces found their voices through the divine—a pantheon inhabited by goddesses who wove the fabric of existence itself. Here, we'll introduce you to some of the most revered and enigmatic figures in Celtic mythology.

Danu, The Earthly Mother

In the heart of Celtic mythology, amidst the rolling hills and lush landscapes, stands Danu, a figure of profound significance. She is the ancestral mother, the divine matriarch from whom the Celts claim their lineage, the representation of the very generative power of the earth itself.

Danu is more than a goddess; she is the embodiment of the earth's life-giving force. Imagine her as the rich, fertile soil from which all life emerges. In her embrace, seeds sprout, creatures thrive, and the world blossoms into its full glory. Her influence is not a distant, ethereal concept but a tangible, nurturing force that sustains everything.

The Nurturer of All Life

Danu's presence in Celtic culture sets a profound tone of reverence for feminine divinity. She is the ultimate nurturer, the mother who feeds her children from her very essence. Her embrace is a sanctuary, a source of boundless love and nourishment. In her, the Celts found not only the giver of life but also a symbol of care, compassion, and protection.

The Essence of Ancestry

The Celts, like many ancient cultures, understood the importance of lineage and heritage. Danu, as the ancestral mother, was the foundation upon which their sense of identity was built. She was a reminder of their deep-rooted connection to the land, the source of their sustenance and culture. To honor Danu was to honor their own ancestry and the enduring spirit of their people.

A Living Legacy

Even today, the echoes of Danu's presence can be felt in Celtic communities. She continues to symbolize the enduring power of the earth, the sanctity of life, and the importance of nurturing and caring for one another and the world around us. Danu's legacy reminds us that, like the Celts of old, we too are stewards of the earth, responsible for its well-being and the well-being of future generations. She is a testament to the deep connection between the Celts and the land they called home, a connection that continues to inspire and guide us in our modern world.

Brigid: A Goddess of Multifaceted Talents

In the pantheon of Celtic goddesses, Brigid stands as a shining example of versatility and multifaceted divinity. Her domain spans across poetry, healing, and smithcraft, encompassing a wide spectrum of roles and attributes. But what truly sets Brigid apart is her embodiment of the myriad roles that women played in Celtic society. She is not confined to a singular aspect of life or femininity; instead, she personifies the rich diversity of women's contributions to their communities.

The Poetic Muse

Brigid's association with poetry is a testament to the profound respect the Celts held for the spoken and written word. In her, they found inspiration, the muse who kindled the flames of creativity in bards and storytellers. She is the driving force behind the lyrical verses that celebrated heroes, chronicled history, and stirred the hearts of listeners. As the goddess of poetry, she elevated language to an art form and ensured that the voices of the Celts would resonate through the ages.

The Healer's Touch

Beyond poetry, Brigid's influence extended to the realm of healing. She was the patroness of physicians and those skilled in the medicinal arts. Her gentle yet powerful presence was sought in times of illness and injury, as she possessed the knowledge and compassion to mend both body and spirit. Through Brigid, the Celts acknowledged the invaluable role of healers, often women, in their communities, and the importance of nurturing health and well-being.

The Smith's Craft

In yet another facet of her divinity, Brigid presided over smithcraft, the art of forging and creation. Here, she embodied the spirit of craftsmanship and innovation. Blacksmiths and artisans, often men and women alike, looked to her for guidance and inspiration in their endeavors. Brigid's domain over smithcraft highlighted the integral role of creators and inventors in Celtic society, forging not just tools and weapons but also the foundations of progress and civilization.

A Mosaic of Roles

Brigid's multifaceted nature as a goddess mirrors the variety of roles women played in Celtic communities. From healers tending to the sick to bards weaving tales of heroism, from warriors defending their land to creators shaping their world, women were integral to every aspect of Celtic life. Brigid's presence served as a reminder that women were not limited by societal boundaries but were, in fact, the driving force behind the cultural, artistic, and healing traditions of the Celts.

In embracing Brigid, we gain insight into the profound respect and recognition the Celts had for the multifaceted roles of women in their society. Her legacy endures as a celebration of the diverse talents and contributions of women, and as an acknowledgment that femininity is a force that can shape, heal, and inspire in countless ways.

Morrígan: The Enigmatic Goddess of Duality

In the pantheon of Celtic goddesses, few embody the complexity and enigma of *Morrígan*. She is a figure of paradox, a deity who personifies the intricate dance of opposing forces that underpins the Celtic worldview. To understand Morrígan is to grasp the profound duality that is woven into the very fabric of nature and life itself.

The Harbinger of Battle

One facet of Morrígan's nature is her role as the harbinger of battle. She is often depicted as a foreboding presence on the battlefield, soaring above in the form of a crow or raven. Her eerie cries were believed to signal imminent conflict and death. While this might seem dark and foreboding, it is a testament

74

to the Celts' acknowledgment of the inevitability of conflict and the ever-present specter of mortality. Morrígan, in this aspect, serves as a reminder of the harsh realities of life and the impermanence of all things.

The Guardian of Sovereignty

Conversely, Morrígan is also revered as the guardian of sovereignty, a role that showcases the flip side of her duality. In this aspect, she is a protector of the land and its rulers. Celtic kings were believed to derive their authority from the goddess, and her favor ensured the prosperity and harmony of the kingdom. This facet of Morrígan underscores the Celts' deep connection to the land and their belief in the cyclical nature of power, where the old must give way to the new for renewal and growth to occur.

The Dance of Destruction and Renewal

Morrígan's dual roles illustrate the profound interplay between destruction and renewal that defines the natural world. In Celtic cosmology, the changing of seasons, the life and death of plants and animals, and the ebb and flow of power were all seen as part of an eternal cycle. Morrígan embodies this cycle, reminding the Celts that, just as battles are followed by peace, and rulers are succeeded by successors, all aspects of life are subject to this cosmic dance of transformation.

A Mysterious Presence

Morrígan's mystery lies not only in her duality but also in her inscrutability. She is a figure of few words, often revealing her intentions through symbols and omens. Her capricious nature keeps both mortals and deities on their toes, for her favor can bring fortune or adversity. This enigmatic quality adds to her allure, emphasizing that the forces of nature and destiny are beyond human comprehension.

Morrígan, with her intricate blend of darkness and light, destruction and renewal, mystery and revelation, embodies the very essence of Celtic goddesses. She is a mirror reflecting the complexities of the world and the understanding that, in embracing these complexities, one gains insight into the profound truths of existence itself.

Cerridwen: The Mysterious Goddess of Transformation

Within Celtic mythology, woven with threads of mysticism, wisdom, and the ever-turning wheel of fate, there exists a figure of profound complexity and significance — Cerridwen. She stands as a guardian of ancient wisdom, a weaver of transformative tales, and a keeper of the Cauldron of Transformation. Her story is a testament to the intricate dance of opposing forces that defines the Celtic worldview, where darkness and light, death and rebirth, and the mortal and divine intertwine.

The Cauldron of Transformation

At the heart of Cerridwen's myth lies her most cherished possession, the Cauldron of Transformation. This mystical vessel possesses the power to brew a potion of profound insight and inspiration, known as 'greal' in Welsh. But this is no ordinary elixir; it carries the potential for personal transformation, an alchemical metamorphosis of the spirit and intellect that can elevate a mortal into a realm of divine wisdom. The legend of Cerridwen and her cauldron embodies the belief that even in the darkest of circumstances, renewal and enlightenment are attainable.

A Guardian of Ancient Wisdom

Cerridwen's role extends beyond the mystical brew of the cauldron. She is revered as a guardian of ancient wisdom, a font of knowledge that transcends the boundaries of time and mortality. Her enigmatic presence serves as a reminder that the forces of life, death, and rebirth are interconnected and that, in embracing their complexities, one gains insight into the profound truths of existence itself.

A Story of Duality and Transformation

Cerridwen's myth illuminates the intricate dance between opposing forces, much like the ever-changing seasons or the cyclical rise and fall of empires. She embodies the duality that underpins the natural world and human experience, where destruction and renewal are two sides of the same coin. Through her tale, we delve into the heart of Celtic mythology, where mysteries are unraveled, and profound insights into the human condition are revealed.

In the Heart of Cerridwen's Myth

Once upon a time, in the ancient land of Wales, there lived a powerful and enigmatic sorceress named Cerridwen. She possessed knowledge beyond the comprehension of mortals, and her dwelling was nestled deep within the lush forests of the region.

Cerridwen's most prized possession was her magical cauldron, known far and wide as the Cauldron of Transformation. This mystical vessel held within it the power to brew a potion of profound insight and inspiration, referred to as 'greal' in Welsh.

This 'greal' was no ordinary brew; it held the potential for personal transformation. Those who partook in its elixir underwent a metamorphosis of the spirit and intellect, transcending the boundaries of the mortal realm to attain divine wisdom.

A Quest for Transformation

Legend has it that Cerridwen's cauldron was no mere relic; it was the crucible of life itself. In its depths, experiences both bitter and sweet would blend to create the elixir of understanding. But this precious potion was not easily obtained.

The Tale of Gwion Bach

One fateful day, Cerridwen decided to brew the 'greal,' entrusting its preparation to a young boy named Gwion Bach. Little did she know that this choice would set in motion a series of events that would forever alter the course of their lives.

As the cauldron bubbled and simmered, Gwion Bach, in a moment of haste, accidentally spilled three drops of the potion onto his finger. Instinctively, he placed his finger in his mouth, and with that, he gained the wisdom and knowledge meant for another.

Realizing the potency of the elixir, Cerridwen pursued Gwion Bach with relentless determination. Their chase took them through various forms, from hare to fish to bird, as they traversed the fabric of time and existence.

The Transformation

Ultimately, Gwion Bach transformed into a grain of wheat and was consumed by Cerridwen in her pursuit. But the story does not end there, for Cerridwen, in consuming the grain, became pregnant. She gave birth to a child named Taliesin, who would become one of the greatest bards and poets of Welsh legend, gifted with the wisdom of the 'greal.'

In this intricate tale of Cerridwen, her cauldron, and the pursuit of wisdom, we find profound symbolism and significance. The cauldron represents not only the transformative power of knowledge but also the crucible of life itself, where experiences, both bitter and sweet, blend to create the elixir of understanding.

As we explore the depths of Cerridwen's story, we come to understand the profound Celtic belief in the potential for renewal, rebirth, and the enduring quest for wisdom that defines the human experience.

Now, let's delve deeper into the tale to understand why this cauldron held such immense significance.

The Symbolism of the Cauldron

The cauldron wasn't just a mundane cooking vessel; it symbolized something profound. In Celtic mythology, it represented not only the transformative power of knowledge but also the crucible of life itself. Just as metals are melted and refined in a crucible, so too are human experiences—both the bitter and the sweet—blended in the cauldron of existence to create the elixir of understanding.

Celtic Goddesses and Nature's Bounty

To understand Celtic goddesses fully, one must recognize their deep connection to the natural world. The Celts, as an agrarian society, depended on the land's fertility for their survival. Thus, the goddesses came to embody the cycles of nature, the changing seasons, and the bounty of the earth.

Danu, as the mother of the Tuatha Dé Danann, represents the fecundity of the land and its ability to sustain life. Brigid's association with the hearth and the forge mirrors the transformative power of nature—where raw materials are turned into tools and sustenance. And Morrígan, with her ties to sovereignty, reflects the land's role in empowering leaders and maintaining balance.

Exploring the Diverse Roles and Attributes

Celtic goddesses were not one-dimensional figures but multifaceted beings who embraced diverse roles and attributes. As we delve deeper, we'll uncover their roles as protectors, healers, and inspirations.

In the guardian aspect, goddesses like Brigid watched over the land, its people, and its creatures. They were the keepers of sacred sites, ensuring that the spiritual connection between the Celts and their environment remained unbroken.

The healing aspect is embodied by goddesses like Airmid, associated with herbalism and the restorative powers of nature. Their presence underscores the Celtic belief in the interconnectedness of physical and spiritual well-being.

As muses and inspirations, goddesses like Brigid ignited the creative flames of poets and artisans. They were the source of inspiration for the bards, who wove tales and songs that celebrated the beauty and mysteries of the world.

The Celtic goddesses, were not mere characters in a story but timeless embodiments of nature, wisdom, and the feminine spirit. Through their stories, it is unveiled a profound connection between the Celts and the land they held sacred, and how these goddesses continue to inspire awe and reverence in the modern world.

Warrior Queens and Goddesses of Sovereignty

At the core of Celtic mythology lies the concept of goddesses who personify the land and its rulers—goddesses of sovereignty. These powerful beings weren't just divine; they held the fate of kingdoms in their hands. In this section we'll explore the fascinating world of warrior queens and sovereignty goddesses, where the lines between myth and reality blur.

Sovereignty Goddesses: Divine Connections to Celtic Kingship

Imagine a realm where the land and its ruler were inextricably linked—a realm where the very soil beneath a king's feet echoed with the pulse of the goddess herself. Celtic kingship wasn't just about political power; it was about divine right. At the heart of this belief system were sovereignty goddesses, enigmatic beings who personified the land and its abundance.

These goddesses were the ultimate authorities, bestowing their favor on chosen leaders and withdrawing it from those who faltered. To understand the significance of warrior queens, we must first grasp the pivotal role these goddesses played in Celtic societies.

Profiles of Notable Warrior Queens

From the mists of time emerge the stories of remarkable women who ruled with strength, wisdom, and grace. These warrior queens were not just historical figures; they were living embodiments of sovereignty goddesses.

Boudicca, The Warrior Queen Who Defied an Empire

In the swirling mists of ancient Britannia, there arose a queen whose name would echo through the annals of history - Boudicca. She was no ordinary monarch. Boudicca was the ruler of the Iceni tribe, a Celtic people who dwelled in the eastern part of the island.

During the first century AD, when the Roman Empire extended its grasp far and wide, Britannia became one of its prized conquests. The Romans had established dominion over the land, imposing their rule with an iron fist. The Iceni had accepted Roman rule, albeit uneasily, hoping to maintain their way of life.

But when Boudicca's husband, Prasutagus, the king of the Iceni, passed away, the uneasy truce between the Iceni and the Romans unraveled. The Romans, in an act of appalling greed, seized the opportunity to strip the Iceni of their lands and possessions. They trampled upon their traditions and dignity, fanning the flames of resentment.

Boudicca, however, was not one to yield to oppression. She rose with a spirit aflame with indignation, rallying her people to defy the Roman oppressors. Her rallying cry was not just a call to arms; it was a fervent plea for justice and the preservation of her people's honor.

The Iceni, joined by other tribes who shared in their suffering, united under Boudicca's leadership. With her at the helm, they became an unstoppable force, determined to reclaim their freedom and dignity from the iron grip of Rome.

In AD 60 or 61, Boudicca and her army clashed with the mighty legions of Rome. The battleground was the ancient city of Camulodunum, modern-day Colchester. The clash was cataclysmic. Boudicca's forces, fierce and passionate, initially seized victory as Camulodunum fell to the rebels. However, their triumph was short-lived as they were ultimately outmatched by the disciplined Roman soldiers.

The Roman governor at the time, Gaius Suetonius Paulinus, swiftly mustered his troops. In a decisive confrontation, Boudicca's rebellion was crushed. The queen herself faced defeat but refused to submit to Roman capture. Legend has it that she consumed poison rather than allowing herself to be paraded as a captive.

Boudicca's story, though marked by tragedy in the end, symbolizes the unwavering spirit of resistance against tyranny. Her courage, resilience, and fierce determination have etched her name in the annals of Celtic history as a warrior queen who defied an empire, fighting not just for her people's freedom but for their honor and dignity. She remains an enduring symbol of resistance against oppression, a beacon of hope for all who cherish the spirit of independence and justice.

Medb - The Ambitious Queen of Connacht

In the verdant landscapes of ancient Ireland, a queen rose to power, leaving an indelible mark on Celtic mythology. Medb, the queen of Connacht, was no ordinary ruler. She was a woman of unyielding ambition, whose name would become synonymous with power, cunning, and a relentless pursuit of her desires. While we briefly touched upon Medb's ambition and the legendary tale of the Brown Bull in the previous section, let us now embark on a deeper exploration of this captivating legend.

The story begins with a seemingly innocuous dispute between Medb and her husband, King Ailill. They were both formidable rulers, and their marriage was built on an unusual foundation of equality. However, a fateful conversation revealed a rift in their partnership, a rift that would set off a chain of events with far-reaching consequences.

In a boastful exchange, the royal couple compared their assets. Ailill, confident in his stature, claimed to possess a prized white bull, a symbol of wealth and prestige. Medb, determined not to be outdone, realized that she lacked an equal treasure in her own lands. This revelation ignited a fire within her, a fire that would drive her to extraordinary lengths to rectify the perceived imbalance.

Medb's ambition knew no bounds. She set her sights on the Brown Bull of Cooley, a magnificent creature that resided in the neighboring kingdom of Ulster. It was a daring move, for Ulster was home to fierce warriors, including the mighty Cú Chulainn. However, Medb was undeterred.

She mobilized her forces, embarking on a ruthless quest to steal the Brown Bull of Cooley. The epic Táin Bó Cúailnge chronicles her relentless pursuit, a tale of cunning and audacity as she sought to claim the prized bull as her own. Her determination was unshakable, even in the face of formidable obstacles and fierce resistance.

Medb's story is a testament to the complexities of power and ambition. She was a ruler who defied convention, challenging traditional gender roles and expectations. Her unyielding pursuit of her goals, even when they led to conflict and chaos, showcases the depths to which a leader could go to assert dominance.

In Medb, we find a character who is both fascinating and enigmatic, a woman who left an indelible mark on Celtic mythology as a symbol of ambition, power, and the unrelenting pursuit of one's desires. Her legacy, as depicted in the Táin Bó Cúailnge, continues to intrigue and captivate audiences, inviting us to ponder the complexities of leadership and the lengths to which individuals are willing to go to fulfill their ambitions.

How These Women Wielded Power

To understand the significance of warrior queens, we must examine how they wielded power in Celtic societies. They weren't just consorts to kings; they were political players, military strategists, and symbols of authority.

As military leaders, these queens commanded armies and led their people into battle. Their martial prowess and strategic acumen were critical to the defense of their realms.

As political figures, they navigated the intricacies of diplomacy and alliance-building. Their decisions could shape the destiny of entire kingdoms.

As symbols of authority, they embodied the sovereignty of the land. Their union with kings was a sacred rite, signifying the divine right to rule.

Gwenhwyfar - The Queen and Her Choices

In the legendary court of Camelot, Gwenhwyfar, often known as Guinevere, held a position of unparalleled influence. As the queen, she embodied grace, beauty, and the ideal of courtly love. Yet, beneath the veneer of regal elegance, Gwenhwyfar's story is one of personal desires and the profound impact they can have on a kingdom.

At the heart of Gwenhwyfar's tale lies a complex web of relationships and choices. She was the beloved wife of King Arthur, a monarch renowned for his wisdom and chivalry. However, her heart was torn between her devotion to the king and her burgeoning feelings for Lancelot, one of Arthur's most trusted knights.

The love triangle between Gwenhwyfar, Arthur, and Lancelot would become a central theme in Arthurian legends, shaping the destiny of Camelot itself. Gwenhwyfar's choices and the consequences that followed illuminate the intricate dance between personal desires and political obligations.

Gwenhwyfar's predicament was not merely a matter of the heart; it was a reflection of the complexities of leadership and the burden of queenship. As queen, she was expected to uphold the ideals of Camelot, including loyalty, honor, and fidelity. Yet, her heart led her down a different path.

Her forbidden love for Lancelot, a knight of unparalleled valor and charm, tested her commitment to her husband and her kingdom. It also sowed the seeds of discord within the court of Camelot, threatening the very foundation of Arthur's reign.

The consequences of Gwenhwyfar's choices were far-reaching. They led to conflict, betrayal, and ultimately, the downfall of Camelot itself. The love affair between Gwenhwyfar and Lancelot, while passionate and profound, proved to be a double-edged sword, one that would cut deeply into the heart of Arthur's realm.

Gwenhwyfar's story serves as a poignant reminder of the intricate interplay between personal desires and the responsibilities of leadership. Her character is not easily defined; she is neither a villain nor a victim but a woman torn between her heart's yearnings and the demands of her position.

In Gwenhwyfar, we find a queen whose choices reverberate through the annals of Arthurian legend, reminding us that even in the realm of myth and legend, the human heart is a force that can shape the destiny of kingdoms and the course of history. Her story continues to captivate our imaginations, inviting us to explore the timeless question of love, loyalty, and the consequences of the choices we make.

Women in Celtic Society - Unveiling Their Empowerment

As we journey deeper into the heart of Celtic mythology and history, we encounter a society where the roles of women were as divers. In Celtic society, women were far from passive observers. They occupied roles that spanned the spectrum from queens and warriors to healers and spiritual leaders. Understanding the status and roles of women in this rich tapestry of culture and tradition is essential to comprehending the depth of Celtic society.

Celtic Legal Systems and Women's Rights

Laws are the backbone of any society, and Celtic legal systems were no exception. What sets Celtic laws apart is the remarkable degree of gender equality they often upheld. Women in Celtic communities had rights and responsibilities that were enshrined in legal codes, providing them with a level of empowerment not always found in other ancient cultures.

Women in Celtic society were more than just property or dependents. Instead, they were active participants in legal proceedings, inheritance, and marriage.

Celtic legal codes, etched in stone and inked onto ancient parchments, embody this ethos of inclusion and respect for women. Here, the past speaks to us, revealing a society where women's voices carried weight and authority.

Guardians of Celtic Wisdom

In Celtic society, women assumed a role of paramount significance - they were the torchbearers of tradition, the custodians of ancient knowledge, and the storytellers who wove the very fabric of their culture.

Within the oral traditions of the Celts, where the spoken word held immeasurable power, women stood as the primary architects of continuity. Through their voices, the echoes of Celtic myths and legends traversed generations, transcending the boundaries of time. These stories weren't mere tales; they were living vessels of Celtic identity.

The narratives of Celtic goddesses and warrior queens will illuminate the pivotal role women played in this delicate dance of cultural preservation. These tales reveal how, against the backdrop of ever-changing eras, women remained the steadfast guardians of the essence of Celtic society, ensuring that the flame of tradition burned brightly, undiminished by the passage of time.

Celebrating Celtic Women

In the rich mosaic of Celtic mythology and history, women emerge as formidable figures who defied conventions, preserved traditions, and shaped their societies. From the divine presence of goddesses to the mortal strength of warrior queens, their roles were diverse and influential. These women, as keepers of wisdom and agents of change, continue to inspire with their enduring legacy.

Chapter 5. Celtic Pagan Rituals and Ceremonies

Within the essence of Celtic Paganism, beneath ancient canopies of trees and amidst the whispering winds, rituals and ceremonies unfold. These sacred practices are the lifeblood of a tradition as old as the land itself, a tradition that weaves the human spirit into the very fabric of nature. Celtic Pagan rituals stand as profound expressions of devotion, connection, and reverence for the natural world.

Connecting with Nature in Celtic Rituals

Central to Celtic Paganism is the belief that the land, the rivers, and the forests possess spirits, consciousness, and divinity. This intrinsic connection with nature sets Celtic rituals apart from many other ancient traditions, even those of neighboring lands. While rituals in Norse Paganism, for instance, often embrace the fierce power of the elements, Celtic rituals lean gently into the harmonious embrace of nature's rhythms. It's here that we find both the unique character and the enduring allure of Celtic Pagan ceremonies.

The Ritual of the Sacred Grove

In the dense heart of the ancient Celtic forests, there existed sacred groves, hallowed realms where the boundaries between the earthly and spiritual realms blurred. The Celts believed that within these groves, they could commune with the spirits of the land and the ancestors who had come before them.

To partake in this sacred ritual, the Celts would gather at the grove during the most auspicious times, often during lunar phases or significant celestial events. They would adorn themselves with garlands of leaves and flowers, symbolizing their interconnectedness with nature.

As the sun dipped below the horizon, the Druids, the spiritual leaders of Celtic society, would lead the congregation in chants and songs, calling upon the spirits to join them. In these ancient woods, the Celts felt the presence of the divine more keenly, their senses attuned to the whispers of the rustling leaves and the murmurs of the forest.

The Ceremony of the Four Elements

The Celts recognized the four elements - Earth, Water, Air, and Fire - as fundamental forces that shaped the world. In their rituals, they sought to harmonize with these elements to maintain balance and harmony in their lives.

During this ceremony, individuals would stand at the edge of a sacred circle, each cardinal point representing one of the elements. To connect with Earth, they would touch the ground, feeling the solid soil beneath their fingers. Water was represented by a flowing stream or pool of water, where participants would cleanse themselves. For Air, they would breathe deeply, letting the winds carry away any negativity. And Fire, the element of transformation, was invoked through a controlled blaze, often within a stone circle.

In this way, the Celts celebrated their profound relationship with nature, affirming their bond with the elements that sustained life. These rituals were not mere observances but deeply spiritual experiences that reinforced their place within the natural world.

Druidic Ceremonies

Druids played a significant role in Celtic Paganism, serving as priests, scholars, and spiritual guides. Their ceremonies often involved communing with nature and the spirits of the land. A notable ritual was the "Ovate Rite," a ceremony to seek guidance and wisdom from the spirits of the forest. Druids would also conduct ceremonies during solstices and equinoxes, celebrating the changing seasons and the cyclical nature of life.

As we delve deeper into the world of Celtic Pagan rituals, we encounter the Ovate Rite, a ceremony that, at first glance, may bear similarities to the Ritual of the Sacred Grove, which we explored earlier. However, it's essential to recognize that while these two rituals share some common elements, they also boast distinct characteristics that set them apart within the rich tapestry of Celtic Pagan practices.

In summary, the Ovate Rite is a distinct ceremony deeply rooted in Celtic Paganism, particularly within the Druidic tradition. It serves as a focused practice for divination, healing, and communing with the spirits of nature. Within this rite, seekers pursue wisdom, establish connections with the living energies of the land, and utilize divinatory tools, such as the ogham, to gain profound insights.

Conversely, the Ritual of the Sacred Grove represents a broader ritual conducted within revered natural settings, known as sacred groves, central to Celtic Pagan reverence. This ceremony encompasses various aspects, including the veneration of nature spirits and deities. It is important to note that while the Ritual of the Sacred Grove may involve these aspects, it does not necessarily incorporate the specific practices and focus of the Ovate Rite. Each holds its unique place within the tapestry of Celtic Paganism.

Ovate Rite: This ritual was particularly focused on seeking guidance and wisdom from the spirits of the forest and the natural world. It often took place in secluded groves or other areas of untouched nature, believed to be places where the veil between the physical and spiritual realms was thin.

Purpose: The Ovate Rite aimed to connect with the spirits of the land and the ancestors, seeking insights into important matters such as governance, agriculture, and personal life decisions.

Ceremony: Druids would gather in a circle within the sacred grove, and a ceremonial fire would be lit. Offerings of food, herbs, or symbolic objects were presented to the spirits. The Druid leading the ceremony would enter a meditative state, often aided by chanting or drumming, to facilitate communication with the spiritual realm.

Divination: During the Ovate Rite, Druids often practiced divination techniques like scrying (gazing into reflective surfaces), reading the patterns of smoke or flames, or interpreting the sounds of the natural world. These divinations were considered messages from the spirits and were used to provide guidance to the community.

Seasonal Significance: The Ovate Rite was often performed during solstices, equinoxes, or other significant points in the agricultural and celestial calendar. These rituals were aligned with the changing seasons and the cyclical nature of life.

Ancestor Veneration: Embracing Ancestral Wisdom

In the heart of Celtic Paganism lies a profound reverence for the wisdom and guidance of those who came before. Ancestor veneration, a central practice in this ancient belief system, encapsulates the Celtic understanding of the interconnectedness of life, death, and the spiritual realm.

Creating Sacred Spaces

Celtic Pagans would often dedicate special areas or altars within their homes or in nature to their ancestors. These sacred spaces served as focal points for rituals and remembrance. They were adorned with meaningful symbols, photographs, or personal items that held significance for the family or individual.

Offerings of Remembrance

An essential element of ancestor veneration was the offering of gifts to one's forebears. These offerings, often consisting of food, drink, or symbolic items, were believed to nourish the spirits of the departed and strengthen the bond between the worlds. The choice of offerings was deeply personal, reflecting the unique relationship between the living and their ancestors.

Seeking Guidance and Protection

Celtic Pagans turned to their ancestors not only to honor their memory but also to seek guidance and protection. Rituals involved heartfelt prayers and invocations, asking for insights into life's challenges or protection from malevolent forces. It was believed that the spirits of the ancestors, having journeyed beyond the mortal realm, possessed a deeper understanding of life's mysteries.

The Rite of the Ancestral Mound

This ritual took place at ancient burial mounds, which were considered places where the veil between the living and the deceased was thinnest. Families would gather at these mounds during significant times of the year, such as the Celtic festival of Samhain.

As dusk settled, torches were lit to illuminate the surroundings, casting flickering shadows upon the ancient stones. The Druids, keepers of spiritual wisdom, would lead the ceremony. They believed that during this time, the spirits of the ancestors would return to commune with the living.

In a solemn procession, participants would approach the burial mound, each holding a small offering of food, drink, or personal mementos. These offerings were meant to sustain and comfort the spirits on their journey back to the earthly realm.

Standing before the mound, the Druids would lead the assembly in chants and invocations, inviting the ancestors to share their wisdom and blessings. This ritual served not only to honor those who had come before but also to seek guidance and protection for the challenges that lay ahead.

The Celts deeply understood the interconnectedness of life and death, viewing the spirits of their ancestors as a wellspring of knowledge and strength. Through the Ancestral Mound ceremony, they celebrated this profound bond, reinforcing their sense of belonging in a lineage that stretched back through the ages.

The Continuity of Life

At its core, ancestor veneration reinforced the Celtic belief in the cyclical nature of existence. Death was not the end but a transition to another state of being. Through these rituals, the living affirmed their connection to those who had passed on, finding comfort in the idea that their loved ones continued to watch over and guide them.

A Living Tradition

In the modern Celtic Pagan revival, the practice of ancestor veneration remains a vibrant and cherished aspect of spirituality. It serves as a reminder that the wisdom and love of our ancestors continue to flow through the currents of time, offering solace, insight, and a profound sense of belonging in a world deeply rooted in tradition and spirituality.

By embracing ancestor veneration, Celtic Pagans celebrate not only their heritage but also the enduring bond between the living and the departed. It is a practice that enriches the soul, reconnects individuals with their roots, and reaffirms the timeless wisdom of the Celtic way of life.

Divination in Celtic Paganism

Divination held a special place within Celtic Paganism, serving as a means of bridging the mortal world with the mystical realm of spirits and deities. This practice allowed Celtic Pagans to seek guidance, unravel mysteries, and understand the hidden currents of fate that flowed through their lives. The methods employed in divination were as diverse as the natural world they revered, each with its unique symbolism and rituals.

Scrying: Gazing into the Otherworld

One of the most intriguing forms of divination among Celtic Pagans was scrying, a practice that involved gazing into reflective surfaces to perceive messages from the Otherworld. Mirrors, pools of water, or even polished stones were often used as scrying tools. The practitioner would enter a meditative state, their eyes fixed upon the surface, allowing the mind to open to the visions and symbols that appeared. These visions were believed to be messages from the spirits, the ancestors, or the deities.

Casting Lots and Runes: The Language of Fate

Another method of divination was casting lots or reading runes. The Celts had their own systems of symbols and glyphs, and these were used to interpret the patterns and combinations that emerged when lots or runes were cast. Each symbol carried profound meaning, often connected to the natural world, mythological stories, or aspects of daily life. By studying the arrangement and relationship between these symbols, Druids and Celtic seers could provide insights into matters of significance, whether personal or communal.

Interpreting Nature's Signs: The Language of the Land

Celtic Pagans were keen observers of the natural world, and they believed that nature itself could offer messages and guidance. They looked to the flight patterns of birds, the shapes and movements of clouds, the rustling of leaves, or the behavior of animals as omens and signs. These observations were not mere coincidences but rather were seen as direct communications from the spirits inhabiting the land.

Seeking Guidance from Deities: Connecting with the Divine

Divination wasn't solely about understanding the mundane aspects of life; it was also a way to connect with the Celtic deities and seek their counsel. Practitioners would often invoke specific deities associated with wisdom or prophecy, such as Brigid or Lugh, during divination rituals. By doing so, they believed they could tap into the divine wisdom and receive answers to their most pressing questions.

Decision-Making and Problem-Solving

Divination played a practical role in Celtic society. It was used for decision-making in various aspects of life, including matters of governance, agriculture, and personal choices. When faced with dilemmas or uncertainties, Celtic leaders and individuals turned to divination to help them make informed decisions in harmony with the will of the spirits and the flow of destiny.

The Sacred Continuity

The practice of divination was more than a means of seeking answers; it was a profound recognition of the interconnectedness of all things. Celtic Pagans believed that through divination, they participated in a timeless dialogue with the Otherworld, affirming the enduring bond between the mortal realm and the realm of spirits and deities.

By employing these divination methods, Celtic Pagans navigated the intricate tapestry of life, drawing on the wisdom of the land, the spirits, and the divine to illuminate their path. These practices weren't just rituals; they were gateways to a deeper understanding of the world, themselves, and the forces that shaped their destiny.

Rites of Passage: Navigating Life's Sacred Thresholds

Celtic Paganism was deeply intertwined with the ebb and flow of human existence, and it recognized the significance of life's major transitions. Rites of passage played a pivotal role in marking these crucial milestones, guiding individuals from one phase of life to another with reverence, symbolism, and profound meaning.

Birth Rituals: Welcoming New Life into the Circle

Birth was a momentous occasion in Celtic society, and it was celebrated as a sacred event connecting the community, the newborn, and the spirits of the land. Birth rituals were joyous occasions, welcoming the newest member of the tribe into the circle of life. It was believed that each child brought blessings and potential, contributing to the continuity of the community. Parents, family members, and Druids often conducted blessings and ceremonies, invoking protective spirits and deities to watch over the child. This act not only ensured the well-being of the infant but also reinforced the connection between the mortal realm and the realm of the spirits.

Coming of Age: Embracing the Transition to Adulthood

As adolescents transitioned into adulthood, Celtic Paganism marked this transformation with rituals of coming of age. These ceremonies symbolized the passage from youth to maturity and often included tests or challenges that young individuals had to overcome to prove their readiness for adult responsibilities. Initiates might be required to spend time in nature, engage in feats of strength or courage, or demonstrate their knowledge of the tribe's traditions. Successfully completing these trials was a rite of passage, signifying readiness to contribute fully to the community.

Marriage Ceremonies: Uniting Hearts and Spirits
Marriage was a sacred union in Celtic Paganism, symbolizing the harmony between individuals, the community, and the natural world. These ceremonies celebrated love, fertility, and the promise of new life. Druids and community leaders conducted marriage rituals, invoking deities associated with love and family, such as Brigid or Lugh. The couple exchanged vows and often offered symbolic gifts to each other and to the spirits. This act not only solidified their bond but also ensured the blessings of the divine on their union.

Funerary Rites: Honoring the Journey to the Otherworld
Death, as in many cultures, held profound significance in Celtic Paganism. It was seen not as an end but as a transition to another phase of existence. Funerary rituals were conducted with great care and reverence. The deceased were prepared for their journey to the Otherworld, often with elaborate burial customs or cremation ceremonies. Druids and community members performed rites to guide the soul safely to the afterlife, seeking the blessings of ancestral spirits and deities associated with death and the underworld. These rituals reinforced the belief in the cyclical nature of existence, where death was not the final destination but a continuation of the soul's journey.

Sacred Continuity through Life's Passages
These rites of passage in Celtic Paganism were more than mere traditions; they were threads that wove individuals into the rich mosaic of community and spirituality. They reinforced the belief that every life event, from birth to death, was imbued with spiritual significance, connecting individuals to their

ancestors, the natural world, and the divine forces that shaped their destiny.

The Cauldron of Rebirth: A Symbol of Transformation

In Celtic mythology, the Cauldron of Rebirth was said to possess magical properties, including the ability to bring the dead back to life. It represents the cyclical nature of existence, where death is not the end but a stage in the ongoing journey of the soul. This cauldron signifies regeneration and renewal, much like the changing seasons in nature.

Role in Rites of Passage

The Cauldron of Rebirth could be connected to rites of passage, particularly in the context of funerary rituals. It symbolized the idea that, just as life flows in cycles, so does the soul's journey. When a person passed away, it was believed that their soul would be placed into the Cauldron of Rebirth, where it would undergo a transformative process. Afterward, the soul would be reborn into a new life, continuing its journey.

In funerary rituals, the presence of the Cauldron of Rebirth could offer solace to the grieving community, assuring them that death was not the end but a part of the eternal cycle of existence.

The Cauldron in Celtic Paganism Today

Today, some modern practitioners of Celtic Paganism draw inspiration from the Cauldron of Rebirth as a symbol of personal transformation, growth, and renewal. It can be incorporated into rituals or meditative practices to explore themes of rebirth and regeneration in one's own life journey.

Celtic Festivals: Embracing Nature's Rhythms

The profound connection of Celtic Paganism with the natural world finds its most vibrant expression in the festivals and celebrations that mark the Celtic Pagan calendar. These festivities, deeply rooted in the cycles of the Earth and the cosmos, provide a window into the soul of Celtic Paganism.

The Dance of Nature and Spirit

Celtic Pagan festivals are more than just occasions for merriment; they are sacred ceremonies that honor the turning of the seasons, the waxing and waning of the moon, and the dance of life and death. These festivals offer a chance for humans to harmonize with the natural forces, celebrating the unity of spirit and earth.

Celtic Paganism vs. Norse Traditions

While both Celtic and Norse traditions share a profound connection to nature and mythology, they diverge in their approach to ritual and celebration. Norse traditions often lean towards grand feasts, elaborate ceremonies, and epic sagas, reflecting the bold and adventurous spirit of the Viking culture.

In contrast, Celtic Paganism, although equally vibrant, tends to emphasize a more intimate and harmonious communion with the natural world. Celtic festivals often take place in secluded groves, on misty hillsides, or by serene lakes, where the boundary between the physical and spiritual realms is thin. These celebrations are marked by a deep sense of reverence for the land, the ancestors, and the mysteries of the cosmos.

As we explore Celtic Pagan festivals in the pages that follow, we'll witness how these ancient ceremonies unite the human spirit with the pulse of the Earth, fostering a profound sense of belonging and interconnectedness. It's within this context that we'll uncover the magic, wisdom, and timeless beauty of Celtic Pagan festivities.

Samhain: Embracing the Celtic New Year

Among the most iconic and widely celebrated of Celtic Pagan festivals is Samhain, marking the beginning of the Celtic year. Observed from sunset on October 31st to sunset on November 1st, Samhain is a time of profound significance and deep spiritual connection.

The Veil Between Worlds

At Samhain, the Celts believed that the boundary between the living and the spirit world became porous. This allowed for easier communication with departed ancestors and nature spirits. The festival serves as a bridge, connecting the realm of the living with the unseen, where wisdom and guidance could flow freely. For Celtic Pagans, this liminal space represents an opportunity for introspection, divination, and honoring those who came before.

Rituals and Traditions

One of the central rituals of Samhain is the lighting of bonfires, symbolizing the sun's diminishing power and the descent into the darker half of the year. Celts would also place offerings of food and drink on altars or doorstep thresholds, providing sustenance for visiting spirits and ancestors. As a gesture of protection, carved pumpkins or turnips with faces would ward off malevolent entities, giving rise to the modern tradition of jack-o'-lanterns.

Samhain is a time for storytelling, where myths, legends, and ancestral tales are shared around the fire. These stories connect the present with the past, reminding the community of its shared history and cultural identity.

Modern celebrations of Samhain often incorporate elements of Halloween, including costumes and trick-or-treating. However, for Celtic Pagans, the focus remains on honoring the sacred cycles of nature and the continuity of life.

Beltane: Embracing Fertility and Union

In stark contrast to Samhain, Beltane is celebrated at the beginning of May, heralding the arrival of spring. This festival is dedicated to fertility, growth, and the union of the masculine and feminine energies in nature.

Maypole Dancing and Bonfires

One of the most recognizable features of Beltane is the maypole dance. Young people would weave ribbons around a tall pole in intricate patterns, symbolizing the intertwining of male and female energies. Bonfires were also lit to honor the sun's return and to provide protection for the growing crops.

Handfasting Ceremonies

Beltane is a favored time for handfasting ceremonies, which resemble modern weddings. Couples would bind their hands together with ribbons, pledging to spend a year and a day together. After this period, they could choose to renew their commitment or part ways. This tradition was a reflection of the temporary nature of life and relationships, echoing the cyclical themes of Celtic Paganism.

Lughnasadh: The Festival of the First Harvest

Lughnasadh, celebrated on August 1st, marks the beginning of the harvest season. This festival is dedicated to the Celtic god Lugh, a deity associated with light, craftsmanship, and skill.

Competitions and Feasting

Lughnasadh was a time for athletic competitions, including horse racing and martial arts. Communities would gather to celebrate with abundant feasts, dancing, and music. The festival was an occasion to showcase individual and collective skills, acknowledging the importance of labor and craftsmanship in sustaining the community.

Harvest Customs

Harvest rituals included the making of corn dollies, intricate braided figures fashioned from the last sheaf of wheat. These corn dollies represented the spirit of the harvest and were kept until the following year's planting season. They were then plowed back into the soil, ensuring a fruitful crop in the coming year.

Imbolc: The Awakening of Spring

Imbolc, celebrated on February 1st, welcomes the first stirrings of spring. This festival is dedicated to Brigid, the Celtic goddess of poetry, healing, and smithcraft.

Brigid's Crosses and Fire Ceremonies

One of the central customs of Imbolc is the weaving of Brigid's crosses, typically made from reeds. These crosses were placed above doorways to protect homes and livestock. Fire ceremonies were also common, symbolizing the returning warmth and light of the sun.

Brigid's Role in Healing and Creativity

Brigid's association with healing and inspiration made Imbolc a time to seek her blessings for these pursuits. It was also a time for purification and cleansing rituals, preparing the body and spirit for the vitality of spring.

Là Fhèill Brìghde: Imbolc in Gaelic Tradition

In Gaelic tradition, Imbolc is known as Là Fhèill Brìghde, dedicated to the Gaelic goddess Brìghde. Brìghde, like her Celtic counterpart, is associated with healing, poetry, and craftsmanship. This festival marks the beginning of spring, a season of hope and renewal.

Household Blessings

A key element of Là Fhèill Brìghde is the blessing of homes and livestock. People would invite Brìghde into their homes by leaving out a piece of clothing or cloth overnight. These items were believed to be imbued with the goddess's healing energy and would be used to cure ailments throughout the year.

Bride's Bed

Another tradition involved creating a "Bride's Bed" where an effigy of Brìghde or a corn dolly was placed. This symbolic act was meant to welcome the goddess into the home. In some regions, girls would dress a sheaf of oats in clothing and place it near the hearth, symbolizing Brìghde's presence.

Spring Cleaning and Purification

As with the broader Celtic Imbolc, Là Fhèill Brìghde also involves cleansing and purification rituals. People would clean their homes, clearing out the old and making way for the new. Fire played a central role in these rituals, symbolizing the return of warmth and light. In some areas, the ashes from Imbolc fires were spread in the fields to promote fertility.

Modern Celebrations

In modern times, Imbolc/Là Fhèill Brìghde is still celebrated by many Pagans and Wiccans. It's a time for lighting candles, performing divinations, and honoring the creative and healing aspects of Brìghde. Some also create Bride's crosses, similar to Brigid's crosses, as symbols of protection.

Lúnasa: The Festival of Lugh

Lúnasa, celebrated on August 1st, marks the first harvest of the year and is dedicated to the Celtic god Lugh. This festival, also known as Lammas in some traditions, celebrates the abundance of the land and the importance of community.

First Fruits and Baking Bread

One of the central customs of Lúnasa is the offering of the first fruits and grains of the harvest. These offerings, often in the form of bread, were baked with the newly harvested grains and shared among the community. This act symbolized the cycle of planting, growth, and harvest.

Competitions and Games

Lúnasa was a time for games and competitions, reflecting Lugh's role as a warrior god. Communities would gather for athletic contests, dancing, and storytelling. The festival reinforced the bonds between people and their connection to the land.

The Tailteann Games

The Tailteann Games, named after the goddess Tailtiu, were a prominent part of Lúnasa celebrations. These games included various sports, arts, and cultural events. The winner of the games received a prized piece of the first harvest, emphasizing the festival's connection to agriculture.

Pilgrimages to Sacred Sites

In some regions, pilgrimages to sacred hills or ancient stone circles were part of Lúnasa traditions. Climbing these heights and paying respects to the land was a way to show gratitude for the harvest and seek blessings for the coming year's crops.

Yule. Winter and Rebirth of Light

The Winter Solstice, known as Yule in Celtic Paganism, is one of the most important festivals in the Celtic Pagan calendar. It typically falls around December 21st or 22nd in the Northern Hemisphere. This celebration revolves around the themes of light, rebirth, and the triumph of life over darkness.

Significance

Rebirth of the Sun: The Winter Solstice marks the shortest day and longest night of the year. It symbolizes the rebirth of the sun, as from this point onwards, the days begin to grow longer, bringing more daylight. This celestial event is deeply significant to Celtic Pagans, representing the eternal cycle of life, death, and rebirth.

Festival of Light: Yule is often called the "Festival of Light." It's a time for kindling fires, lighting candles, and decorating homes with evergreen plants like holly and mistletoe. These practices are a symbolic gesture to encourage the return of the sun's warmth and light.

Honoring Ancestors: Just as in other Celtic Pagan festivals, the Winter Solstice is a time for honoring ancestors. It's believed that the veil between the physical and spiritual worlds is thin during this time, making it easier to communicate with and pay respects to those who have passed away.

Fertility and Growth: Yule is also associated with fertility and the promise of future growth. Many customs involve the planting of symbolic seeds or the exchange of gifts to represent the bountiful year ahead.

Traditional Practices

Bonfires: Lighting large bonfires is a common practice during Yule celebrations. People gather around these fires to symbolize the returning of the sun's light and to foster a sense of community.

Feasting: Like many other Celtic Pagan festivals, Yule involves feasting with family and friends. Traditional foods such as roast meats, root vegetables, and spiced cakes are often enjoyed.

Gift-Giving: The exchange of gifts is a way to express love and goodwill during Yule. It's a practice that has been adopted in many modern Christmas traditions.

Evergreen Decorations: Decorating with evergreen plants is a way to symbolize the continuity of life and nature's resilience, even in the depths of winter.

The Winter Solstice, or Yule, is a time of reflection, renewal, and hope within Celtic Paganism. It reinforces the interconnectedness of humanity with the natural world and the importance of celebrating life's cyclical nature.

Celtic Festivals: Embracing Nature's Essence

At the essence of Celtic Paganism lies a profound reverence for the natural world and a deep connection with the spirits of the land. The rituals and ceremonies we've explored in this chapter are not mere performances; they are sacred acts that bind practitioners to the rhythms of nature and the wisdom of their ancestors.

Celtic Pagan rituals are a celebration of life's cycles, from birth to death and everything in between. They are a testament to the enduring bond between humanity and the natural world. In these ceremonies, the Celts found solace, guidance, and a profound sense of belonging in a world that was both beautiful and mysterious.

As we've journeyed through the annals of Celtic culture, we've witnessed how these rituals have evolved over time, adapting to changing circumstances and surviving even in the face of external pressures. We've marveled at their diversity, from the quiet introspection of the Ovate Rite to the exuberant festivities of Beltane. So, dear reader, as we leave behind the sacred groves and fire-lit circles of ancient rituals, we carry with us the wisdom of the Celts, a people who knew that in honoring nature, they were also honoring themselves.

Chapter 6 . The Druids Unearthed: Keepers of Celtic Secrets

In the enchanting world of Celtic Paganism, there exist revered figures who bridge the realms of spirituality, knowledge, and nature. These figures are the Druids, often shrouded in mystery, yet central to the tapestry of Celtic spiritual traditions.

The Druids held a sacred duty in Celtic society: the preservation and transmission of ancient wisdom. They were the custodians of knowledge, the bearers of stories, and the guardians of a tradition that linked the Celts to the profound rhythms of the natural world.

Druids embodied a deep connection to the spiritual realms, where the physical world and the unseen domains coexisted harmoniously. In this chapter, we embark on a journey to uncover the multifaceted role of Druids in Celtic Paganism, exploring their wisdom, magic, and their pivotal role as intermediaries between humanity and the divine.

The Druidic Path: Nature and Rituals

Within Celtic Paganism, the Druids walked a path intertwined with the very essence of nature. Their rituals, deeply rooted in the natural world, played a pivotal role in connecting the Celtic people to the divine forces that shaped their lives.

At the heart of Druidic responsibility lay the preservation and evolution of Celtic spiritual practices. They were the architects of ceremonies that celebrated the changing seasons, honored the spirits of the land, and invoked the blessings of the gods. Through their wisdom and knowledge, they kept the flame of Celtic spirituality alive.

Symbolism of Celtic Rituals and Ceremonies

Celtic rituals and ceremonies were not mere rote actions but rather intricate expressions of spiritual significance, deeply interwoven with symbolism drawn from the natural world. The Druids, as the esteemed custodians of these traditions, played a pivotal role in deciphering and imparting the profound meanings behind these rituals.

Sacred Elements: A Deeper Understanding

In Celtic Paganism, the sacred elements of earth, water, fire, and air were more than just fundamental building blocks of the physical world; they were revered sources of spiritual insight and wisdom.

Earth (Talamh)

In Celtic rituals, the element of earth was revered through various practices:

Offerings of Grains and Soil: Druids and practitioners would make offerings of grains, soil, or seeds to honor the earth element. These offerings symbolized gratitude for the land's fertility and the promise of future abundance. Seeds, in particular, held the potential for growth and represented the cycle of life.

Creating Earth Circles: During certain ceremonies, Druids would create circles on the ground using soil or stones. These circles served as sacred spaces, connecting participants to the energies of the earth. Within these circles, rituals, dances, and divinations would take place.

Burying or Planting: The act of burying objects or planting seeds in the earth was a common ritual practice. It symbolized the idea of returning something to the earth, whether as an offering or to symbolize rebirth and transformation. This practice highlighted the cyclical nature of life and death.

Water (Uisce)

Water held a significant role in Celtic rituals, symbolizing purification, emotional connection, and spiritual insight:

Blessings with Water: Druids would bless participants by sprinkling or washing them with consecrated water, often drawn from sacred wells or springs. This act cleansed individuals of negative energies and prepared them for ritual work.

Purification Ceremonies: Before engaging in major rituals or festivals, individuals would undergo purification ceremonies involving water. These ceremonies aimed to cleanse the body, mind, and spirit, ensuring participants were spiritually prepared.

Scrying with Water: Scrying, the practice of gazing into reflective surfaces to gain insights, was particularly associated with water. Druids would use bowls or pools of water for scrying, seeking visions, guidance, and messages from the spirit world. Ripples, reflections, and patterns in the water were interpreted as divinatory signs.

Fire (Tine)

Fire represented transformation, inspiration, and the eternal cycle of life. Celtic rituals involving fire included:

Lighting Sacred Fires: The act of kindling sacred fires was central to many Celtic rituals and festivals, such as Beltane. These fires symbolized the sun's power, the warmth of community, and the transformative energy of fire. Participants often jumped over or walked between bonfires for blessings.

Candle Magic: In smaller, more intimate rituals, candles were often used to represent the element of fire. The flame's dancing light was seen as a connection to the spiritual realms, and practitioners would meditate on the flames or use them to focus their intentions.

Fire Offerings: Offerings to the element of fire included herbs, grains, and sometimes symbolic objects. These offerings were placed in the flames as gifts to the divine or as a way to release intentions and desires into the universe.

Air (Gaoth)

Air represented intellect, communication, and the breath of life. In Celtic rituals, air was invoked through various practices:

Invocation Through Breath: Druids and participants often began rituals by taking deep breaths of the fresh, outdoor air. This practice connected them to the element of air and prepared them for the work ahead.

Incantations and Chants: Spoken or sung words carried the power of air. Druids would use incantations, chants, and spoken invocations to communicate with the spirits, seek blessings, and set intentions. The sound of their voices carried their intentions on the air currents.

Feather and Bird Imagery: Feathers and bird imagery were used in rituals to invoke the qualities of air. Participants might hold feathers, wear bird-inspired symbols, or even mimic bird movements as a way to align with the element's energy.

Animal Totems in Druidic Practice

Celtic Paganism held a profound reverence for the natural world, with animals being regarded as not only companions in the physical realm but also as spiritual guides and symbols of intrinsic qualities. Druids, as the custodians of Celtic spirituality, incorporated these animal totems into their practices in meaningful ways:

Stag (Cervus elaphus): The stag, with its majestic antlers, symbolized strength, virility, and leadership in Celtic culture. Druids often invoked the spirit of the stag in rituals involving personal empowerment, courage, and protection. The stag's energy was believed to infuse participants with resilience and the ability to overcome challenges.

Salmon (Salmo salar): The salmon held a special place in Celtic mythology, embodying wisdom, knowledge, and the pursuit of enlightenment. Druids recognized the salmon's journey upstream as a metaphor for the quest for deeper understanding and spiritual growth. Ceremonies involving the salmon were conducted to seek insight, guidance, and the illumination of hidden truths.

Raven (Corvus corax): The raven was revered for its intelligence, cunning, and connection to the Otherworld. Druids associated the raven with prophecy, divination, and messages from the spirit realm. They often observed the behavior of ravens and considered their presence during rituals as a sign of spiritual significance. Raven-themed ceremonies were conducted to seek foresight and unveil hidden knowledge.

Wolf (Canis lupus): Wolves were seen as symbols of guardianship, loyalty, and the power of the pack. Druids honored the wolf's qualities in ceremonies related to community, protection, and working together harmoniously. Invoking the spirit of the wolf was believed to strengthen bonds among participants and foster a sense of unity.

Horse (Equus ferus caballus): The horse represented freedom, travel, and the journey of the soul. Druids incorporated the horse's energy into rituals involving personal exploration, adventure, and spiritual quests. The horse's spirit was invoked to guide individuals on transformative journeys and facilitate personal growth.

These animal totems were not merely symbols but were considered as living embodiments of spiritual qualities. Druids would often meditate upon these totems, seek their guidance in dreams, or use their symbolism in divination practices. Furthermore, these totems were featured in ritual artwork, such as carvings, banners, or masks, to evoke their qualities during ceremonies.

Circles and Spirals: Symbols of Eternal Cycles

Within the heart of Celtic Paganism, the sacredness of cycles, both in nature and in the human experience, was profoundly revered. This veneration found expression in the use of circular patterns and spirals as powerful symbols.

Circular Patterns:

The circle, with its seamless, unbroken form, embodied the concept of eternity and the unceasing flow of existence. In Druidic traditions, it was seen as a representation of the cyclical journey of life, death, and rebirth. Rituals conducted within the confines of a sacred circle symbolized the timeless connection between the physical realm and the spiritual world.

Spirals:

Spirals, with their winding, labyrinthine paths, added depth to this symbolism. They signified not only the cyclical nature of existence but also the intricate journey of personal growth and enlightenment. Labyrinths and spiral formations, often carved into stone, marked the hallowed grounds where Druids conducted their ceremonies. These enigmatic patterns served as gateways to the mysteries of the universe, inviting seekers to embark on a transformative journey within.

Triskele and Triskelion: Spirals of Celtic Wisdom

Within the Symbols of the Celtic culture, the triskele and triskelion emerged as potent emblems of transformation, progress, and spiritual evolution.

The Triple Spiral (Triskele)

Cycles and Progress: The triple spiral, often referred to as the triskele, held a central place in Celtic spirituality. It symbolized the cyclical nature of life, death, and rebirth—the eternal flow of existence. For Druids, this emblem represented the interconnectedness of all phases of life and the belief in continuous personal growth and transformation.

Interwoven Phases: The triple spiral's design features three spirals, interwoven and connected, moving both outward and inward. This visual representation signified the ever-evolving journey of the soul. Druids believed that individuals moved through various stages of life, learning, and enlightenment, and the triple spiral beautifully captured this intricate dance of existence.

Spiritual Evolution: In Druidic rituals and ceremonies, the triple spiral was invoked to celebrate life's transitions and acknowledge the soul's progress along its spiritual path. Whether it was a birth, coming of age, marriage, or death, this symbol served as a reminder that each phase was part of a larger cycle and an opportunity for personal and spiritual evolution.

The Triskelion

Sacred Movement: The triskelion, a variant of the triple spiral, featured three distinct legs radiating from a central point. This design suggested dynamic movement and motion. Druids regarded the triskelion as a symbol of forward momentum, emphasizing the importance of embracing change and growth in one's journey.

Navigating Life's Phases: Within Druidic practices, the triskelion represented a compass guiding individuals through life's twists and turns. It was particularly invoked during ceremonies that marked significant transitions, such as initiation rituals or rites of passage, to inspire participants to embrace new chapters in their lives.

Harmony and Balance: The triskelion's balanced and symmetrical form underscored the idea of equilibrium and harmony. Druids believed that by aligning oneself with the natural rhythms of the Earth and the spiritual realms, inner and outer balance could be achieved. This concept was central to their rituals, fostering a sense of unity with nature and the cosmos.

In Druidic ceremonies, both the triple spiral and the triskelion were used as powerful symbols to facilitate a deeper connection with the cycles of life, personal growth, and the ever-flowing currents of the spiritual world. Participants would often meditate upon these symbols, incorporate them into rituals through artwork and adornments, or simply contemplate their profound meanings as they sought wisdom and enlightenment on their spiritual journeys.

Guardians of Sacred Sites

The sacred grove stood as an emblem of the Druidic connection to the natural world. Druids were the stewards of these hallowed places, tending to their spiritual significance and ensuring their sanctity. These groves were more than just physical locations; they were gateways to the divine.

Rituals Within Sacred Spaces

Within the sacred groves, Druids conducted ceremonies that bridged the mortal realm with the spiritual. The ancient trees, standing tall and wise, witnessed the rituals that celebrated life's cycles, sought wisdom from the spirits, and deepened the bonds between the Celtic people and their land.

The Significance of Sacred Sites

The sacred groves, along with other natural sites, held immense importance in Celtic Paganism. They were not merely locations for rituals but embodied the very spirit of the land. These sites were where the Celts communed with their gods, sought guidance from the spirits, and rekindled their reverence for nature.

The Perpetual Flame (Eternal Fire)

In Celtic spirituality, the perpetual flame represents the eternal presence of divine energy and the unbroken connection between the mortal and divine realms. This sacred fire, often tended by Druids or priestesses, symbolized the enduring light of knowledge, protection, and inspiration.

Symbol of Wisdom: The perpetual flame is a beacon of wisdom, signifying the eternal pursuit of knowledge and enlightenment. It was believed that gazing into the flames could reveal hidden truths and inspire profound insights.

Protection and Cleansing: It served as a protective force, warding off negative energies and ensuring the sanctity of sacred spaces. The Celts would often light these flames during important rituals and gatherings.

Connection to Deities: The flame was dedicated to specific deities or spirits, forging a direct connection between the mortal world and the divine. It was a conduit for prayers, offerings, and communication with higher powers.

Sacred Wells

Sacred wells hold a special place in Celtic spirituality, and their significance goes beyond mere sources of water. They are considered thresholds between the physical and spiritual realms, places where the divine and the earthly intersect.

Healing and Purification: These wells were believed to possess healing properties. Pilgrims would visit them seeking physical, emotional, or spiritual healing. Immersing oneself in the waters or leaving offerings was a common practice.

Divination and Prophecy: Like the perpetual flame, sacred wells were also used for divination. It was thought that by gazing into the depths of the well, one could receive insights into the future or guidance from the spirit world.

Gateways to the Otherworld: Many legends tell of sacred wells as entrances to the Otherworld, a realm of spirits and magical beings. They were places where the veil between worlds was thin, allowing for communication with otherworldly entities.

Offerings and Reverence: Offerings such as coins, flowers, or small trinkets were left at these wells as tokens of respect and gratitude to the spirits inhabiting them. This practice reinforced the bond between humans and the natural world.

In contemporary Celtic Paganism and Druidry, the perpetual flame and sacred wells continue to hold deep symbolism. They are often integrated into rituals and ceremonies, serving as reminders of the enduring connection between humanity, the divine, and the natural world. Whether through the eternal flame's wisdom or the sacred well's healing properties, these elements remain potent symbols of Celtic spirituality.

Honoring the Seasons: Druids and Celtic Festivals

Druids, deeply attuned to the natural world, found profound significance in the changing seasons. Their role in Celtic festivals, while previously explored, is worth revisiting through the lens of their unique perspective.

Samhain (End of October):

Samhain, the Celtic New Year, marks the end of the harvest season and the beginning of winter's darkness. Druids played a pivotal role in Samhain ceremonies:

Ancestral Honoring: Samhain was a time to honor and connect with ancestors. Druids led ceremonies where participants offered food, drink, and gifts to spirits and ancestors. These offerings were often placed on altars or at sacred sites.

Divination: Druids used divination practices, such as scrying or reading the patterns of bonfires, to gain insights into the coming year. The thinning of the veil between worlds during Samhain made it an ideal time for seeking guidance from the spirit realm.

Imbolc (Early February):

Imbolc heralds the approach of spring and the return of life to the land. Druids played a role in fertility rites and the celebration of the first stirrings of spring:

Brigid's Blessings: Imbolc was strongly associated with the Celtic goddess Brigid, revered for her connection to healing, poetry, and fire. Druids conducted ceremonies invoking Brigid's blessings for inspiration, creativity, and the healing of land and people.

Lighting of Candles: Candles were lit to symbolize the increasing power of the sun. Druids often performed candlelit rituals, illuminating the darkness of winter and welcoming the returning light.

Beltane (End of April):

Beltane celebrates the full arrival of spring and the awakening of the land's fertility. Druids played key roles in Beltane's festivities:

Maypole Dancing: Maypole dancing was a central feature of Beltane celebrations. Druids led these dances, intertwining ribbons as a symbol of the union between the masculine and feminine energies in nature.

Fire Rituals: Beltane fires were kindled as symbols of the sun's vitality and the warmth of community. Druids conducted fire rituals, and participants often leaped over bonfires for purification and blessings.

Lughnasadh (Early August):

Lughnasadh, also known as Lammas, marks the first harvest and the ripening of grains. Druids had special roles in these agricultural ceremonies:

Harvest Blessings: Druids would bless the first grains and fruits of the season, offering gratitude to the earth for her abundance. These blessings ensured a successful harvest and the well-being of the community.

Games and Competitions: Lughnasadh was associated with the god Lugh, the master of skills. Druids organized and participated in games, contests, and skill demonstrations to honor his spirit and promote unity among the people.

The Bardic Tradition

Druids were not solely focused on rituals and nature; they were also keepers of Celtic culture, language, and history. The Bardic tradition was integral to their role. Bards were poets, storytellers, and musicians who used their art to preserve and transmit knowledge through the generations.

Preservers of Oral Tradition

In a time when writing was rare and knowledge was primarily passed down orally, Druids played a pivotal role in maintaining the cultural identity of the Celtic people. They composed epic poems and songs that recounted the history, mythology, and wisdom of their society.

Oral Versus Written Knowledge

Despite their ability to write in Greek and Latin, Druids were deeply committed to the oral transmission of their most sacred knowledge. They believed that writing down their wisdom would weaken its power and sacredness. Therefore, they relied heavily on memory and oral recitation for their most important teachings.

The Ogham Script

While they may have avoided writing down their spiritual teachings, Druids did employ a script known as Ogham for other purposes. This unique script, consisting of a series of notches or lines carved on stones or sticks, was used for inscriptions and divination. It was often connected with the Druidic art of divining.

The Druidesses

Celtic society was unique in its progressive view of women's roles and contributions. We already discussed how women were not just an integral part of this ancient culture; they held significant positions, including as Druidesses. These women were not merely passive observers but actively participated in religious, spiritual, and social aspects of Celtic life.

Roles of Druidesses

Priestesses: Druidesses held the role of priestesses within the Celtic religious framework. They were guardians of sacred rituals and ceremonies, performing essential religious functions alongside male Druids.

Prophetesses: Much like their male counterparts, Druidesses possessed the gift of clairvoyance and divination. Their prophetic abilities were highly respected, and they played a crucial role in guiding their communities.

Wise Women: Druidesses were known for their wisdom, not just in the spiritual realm but also in herbalism, healing, and various practical aspects of life. They served as advisors and healers, providing invaluable knowledge to their people.

Warriors: Some historical accounts and myths suggest that Celtic women, including Druidesses, actively participated in battles. They were skilled warriors who fought to defend their land and people.

Celtic Druidess Communities

While Druidesses existed in Celtic society, their exact roles and functions can vary depending on regional and cultural differences within the Celtic world. Some historical evidence points to female Druid priestly communities, similar to their male counterparts. These communities often resided on secluded islands, away from male Druids and the rest of society.

One famous example is the mythical island of Avalon, part of the Arthurian legend, which is said to be inhabited by priestesses. Although Avalon is a legend, it reflects the idea of sacred, all-female communities within Celtic culture.

Avalon: The Enigmatic Isle of Druidesses

In the exploration of Druidesses within Celtic society, one famous example emerges from the mists of Celtic mythology—the mythical island of Avalon. This island is most renowned for its association with the Arthurian legends, particularly as the final resting place of King Arthur. However, it's not just the legendary King who is connected to Avalon; the island is also believed to be inhabited by Druidesses.

Avalon, although existing primarily within the realm of myth and folklore, intriguingly reflects the concept of sacred, all-female communities within Celtic culture. The legends surrounding Avalon depict it as a mystical place, veiled in mists and hidden from the ordinary world. It is often described as a sanctuary, a realm where magic and spirituality converge, and where the powerful enchantress, Morgan le Fay, is said to reside. This mysterious island encapsulates the idea of a realm where Druidesses and their mystical practices thrived.

In Arthurian legends, Avalon is where King Arthur is taken to recover from his wounds after the Battle of Camlann. It's also the place where the magical sword Excalibur was forged and later returned after Arthur's death. These elements underscore the island's role as a sacred and magical site.

While Avalon may be a product of myth, its symbolism resonates with the notion of female Druidic communities that were believed to exist in ancient Celtic societies. It reflects the reverence for the sacred feminine and the belief in the unique wisdom and spiritual power of women within Celtic Paganism. The legend of Avalon continues to inspire contemporary interpretations and representations of Druidesses in Celtic spirituality.

Celtic Women: Empowerment and Integration

In summary, Druidesses were vital figures in Celtic Paganism, embodying diverse roles as priestesses, prophetesses, wise women, and even warriors. They contributed significantly to Celtic society, fostering a culture of wisdom, spirituality, and gender equality that continues to resonate in modern interpretations of Celtic spirituality.

Chapter 7. Celtic Spirituality in the Modern World. A Living Tradition

Celtic spirituality is far from a relic of the past; it thrives in the contemporary world, offering wisdom and inspiration to those who seek it. In this final chapter, we'll embark on a journey that bridges the ancient origins of Celtic spirituality with its profound relevance in the present day.

In this chapter, we delve deeper into the heart of Celtic spirituality as a living tradition. We'll explore how it has evolved and adapted to the rhythms of the modern world, how it finds resonance in the lives of individuals, and how it continues to influence and inspire contemporary culture.

So, welcome to the modern Celtic world, where ancient wisdom meets contemporary spirit, and where the legacy of the Celts continues to enrich the lives of those who follow its winding path. This is a world where the past and the present dance together in harmony, where the stories of old find new voices, and where the spirit of the Celts lives on, stronger than ever. Join us on this final journey as we uncover the enduring vitality of Celtic spirituality in the modern world.

Neo-Paganism and Modern Celtic Pagan Paths

In the modern world, Celtic spirituality has found a welcoming embrace within the broader Neo-Pagan movement. Neo-Paganism is a diverse and evolving belief system that draws inspiration from the pre-Christian traditions of Europe, including the Celts. It encompasses a wide array of beliefs, practices, and traditions, making it a multifaceted tapestry that continues to grow and adapt.

The Varied Paths Within

Modern Celtic Paganism is a subset of Neo-Paganism, and it's here that we find a multitude of paths and traditions, each with its own unique approach to connecting with Celtic spirituality. These paths can include:

1. *Druidry:* Inspired by the ancient Druids, modern Druidry is a spiritual practice that emphasizes a deep connection with nature, wisdom, and the pursuit of balance in life. Druids today may be scholars, environmental activists, or individuals deeply attuned to the natural world.

2. *Celtic Reconstructionism:* This approach involves a meticulous study of historical Celtic sources, such as myths, folklore, and ancient texts. It aims to reconstruct and revive the practices and beliefs of the ancient Celts as authentically as possible.

3. *Celtic Wicca:* A blend of Celtic spirituality and Wiccan practices, Celtic Wicca incorporates elements like ritual magic, witchcraft, and a reverence for Celtic deities into its framework.

4. *Eclectic Celtic Spirituality:* Many practitioners prefer a more eclectic approach, drawing inspiration from various Celtic

traditions and blending them with other spiritual practices or beliefs.

Beliefs and Rituals in the Modern Context

In today's society, these modern Celtic Pagan paths continue to evolve. Beliefs often center around the reverence of nature, the interconnectedness of all living things, and the honoring of Celtic deities and spirits. Practices and rituals may include:

1. *Nature-Based Spirituality*: A deep connection to the natural world is a common thread among modern Celtic Pagans. Many rituals and practices revolve around the changing seasons, moon phases, and the cycles of life, death, and rebirth observed in nature.

2. *Ancestor Worship:* Some Celtic Pagans honor their ancestors, seeking guidance and wisdom from those who came before them. This practice underscores the importance of lineage and connection to one's roots.

3. *Ritual Magic:* Spellwork and ritual magic are often incorporated into modern Celtic Paganism. These practices may include divination, meditation, and the crafting of talismans or charms.

4. *Festivals and Celebrations:* Celtic Paganism observes the traditional festivals of the Celtic calendar, such as Samhain, Beltane, and Imbolc. These celebrations mark significant points in the agricultural and spiritual year, and they continue to be observed with reverence and joy.

In the context of today's world, these beliefs, practices, and rituals provide a sense of connection, purpose, and spiritual fulfillment to modern Celtic Pagans. As we explore these paths, we gain insight into how Celtic spirituality remains a vibrant and evolving tradition in the 21st century.

Druidry in the Modern World: Embracing Nature and Wisdom

In the modern era, the ancient practice of Druidry has experienced a resurgence. This revival is marked by a deep reverence for nature, wisdom, and the pursuit of balance in life. Modern Druids find inspiration in the ways of their ancient predecessors, yet adapt these practices to address contemporary challenges and needs.

The Revival of Druidry

The roots of contemporary Druidry trace back to the 18th and 19th centuries when interest in the ancient Celts and their spiritual practices rekindled. This revival was marked by a romantic fascination with nature, folklore, and a desire to reconnect with the natural world.

Modern Druid Roles

One of the defining characteristics of modern Druidry is its diversity in practice and belief. Modern Druids can take on various roles within the community:

Scholars: Some Druids are dedicated to scholarly pursuits, delving into Celtic history, mythology, and ancient texts to gain a deeper understanding of their heritage.

Environmental Activists: Others feel a strong calling to protect and preserve the environment. They view themselves as stewards of the Earth and actively engage in ecological and conservation efforts.

Spiritual Leaders: Many modern Druids embrace their role as spiritual guides and leaders. They conduct rituals, ceremonies, and provide guidance to those seeking a deeper connection with nature and spirituality.

Practices of Modern Druidry

Modern Druidry encompasses a wide range of practices that reflect its core values: Nature-Centric Spirituality, Rituals and Festivals, Community Gatherings.

To provide insight into the practical aspects of modern Druidry, here are a few illustrative examples:

The Order of Bards, Ovates, and Druids (OBOD): This organization, founded in 1964, is one of the largest and most prominent Druidry groups. OBOD offers courses, publications, and gatherings for those interested in Druidry.

Awenyddion: This subset of modern Druidry focuses on the poetic and visionary aspects of the tradition, emphasizing inspiration and creativity.

Eclectic Druids: Some individuals adopt an eclectic approach, incorporating Druidic practices into their own unique spiritual path.

Modern Druidry, with its deep connection to nature and spirituality, continues to evolve, offering individuals a meaningful way to engage with the wisdom of the ancient Celts while navigating the complexities of the modern world.

Celtic Reconstructionism: Reviving Ancient Wisdom with Authenticity

Celtic Reconstructionism is a contemporary movement that is deeply dedicated to authenticity in reviving the ancient Celtic beliefs and practices. At its core, it seeks to reconstruct Celtic spirituality as faithfully as possible based on historical sources and archaeological evidence. Here are some key principles of Celtic Reconstructionism:

Historical Accuracy: A central tenet of Celtic Reconstructionism is an unwavering commitment to historical accuracy. Practitioners rigorously study ancient Celtic texts, folklore, archaeological findings, and historical records to ensure that their practices align with the beliefs and rituals of the ancient Celts.

Respect for Tradition: Celtic Reconstructionists hold a deep respect for the traditions of their ancestors. They strive to preserve the cultural and spiritual heritage of the Celts and avoid incorporating elements from other traditions that may dilute the authenticity of their practices.

Sustainability: Many Celtic Reconstructionists emphasize sustainable and eco-friendly practices, reflecting the ancient Celtic reverence for nature and the environment. They seek to live in harmony with the natural world, just as their ancestors did.

Reconstructing Celtic Beliefs and Practices
Celtic Reconstructionism involves a meticulous process of reconstructing and reviving ancient Celtic beliefs and practices. Here are the key steps in this process:

Research and Study: Celtic Reconstructionists immerse themselves in extensive research and study. They delve into ancient texts, such as the Irish Mythological Cycle, Welsh Mabinogion, and other historical records, to gain insights into the beliefs and rituals of the Celts.

Language and Cultural Studies: Some practitioners also invest in learning ancient Celtic languages, like Old Irish or Old Welsh, to gain a deeper understanding of the linguistic nuances and cultural context of the ancient Celts.

Practical Application: Reconstructionists actively apply their research findings to their spiritual practices. This may involve the recreation of ancient rituals, festivals, and ceremonies.

Prominent Figures and Organizations

The Celtic Reconstructionist movement has seen the contributions of various individuals and organizations committed to its principles:

Erynn Rowan Laurie: Erynn Rowan Laurie is a respected figure in the Celtic Reconstructionist community. She is known for her scholarly work and writings on Celtic spirituality, including the book "A Circle of Stones."

Ár nDraíocht Féin (ADF): Ár nDraíocht Féin, meaning "Our Own Druidry" in Irish, is an organization founded by Isaac Bonewits. While it encompasses a broader Druidic approach, it includes members who are dedicated to Celtic Reconstructionism. ADF offers resources, rituals, and training for those interested in Celtic spirituality.

Clann Bhride: This organization focuses on the veneration of the Irish goddess Brigid and incorporates Celtic Reconstructionist principles into its practices.

Celtic Reconstructionism is a path that demands dedication, scholarly rigor, and a profound commitment to authenticity. Practitioners believe that by faithfully reconstructing the beliefs and practices of their ancestors, they can tap into the wisdom and spirituality of the ancient Celts in a way that is true to their heritage.

Bridging Celtic Spirituality with Wiccan Practices

Celtic Wicca is a modern spiritual path that beautifully merges the rich tapestry of Celtic spirituality with the magical practices of Wicca. It's an eclectic and syncretic tradition that embraces the mystical essence of Celtic traditions while incorporating the rituals, symbolism, and magical techniques commonly associated with Wicca.

Core Beliefs and Rituals

Celtic Wicca shares many foundational beliefs and practices with Wicca while infusing them with Celtic flavor. Here are some core aspects of Celtic Wicca:

Veneration of Celtic Deities: Like their counterparts in Celtic Reconstructionism and Druidry, Celtic Wiccans often honor Celtic deities in their practices. Deities such as Brigid, Cernunnos, Danu, and Lugh hold significant roles in Celtic Wiccan rituals and spellwork.

Cycles of Nature: Celtic Wicca reveres the cycles of nature, much like traditional Celtic spirituality. The Wheel of the Year, a series of eight festivals that mark seasonal changes, is celebrated with reverence. These festivals include Samhain, Beltane, and Imbolc, among others.

Magic and Spellwork: The magical aspect of Celtic Wicca is deeply ingrained in its practices. Rituals often involve spellwork, divination, and the use of magical tools like wands, athames (ritual knives), and candles. Magic is seen as a way to harness natural energies in alignment with one's intentions.

Connection to the Elements: Much like in Druidry, Celtic Wicca acknowledges the significance of the elements - Earth, Air, Fire, and Water - and often incorporates them into rituals and spellwork. Each element holds specific attributes and energies that can be harnessed for various purposes.

Exploring Celtic and Wiccan Traditions

Celtic Wicca practitioners navigate a beautiful blend of two distinct traditions, creating a unique and spiritually enriching experience. Here's how they connect with both Celtic and Wiccan elements:

Honoring Ancestral Roots: Celtic Wiccans pay homage to their Celtic ancestry by incorporating Celtic deities, symbols, and mythology into their rituals. This is a way of connecting with their heritage and embracing the spirituality of their Celtic ancestors.

Wiccan Structure: While Celtic Wicca embraces Celtic elements, it retains the structured framework commonly associated with Wicca. Rituals often follow the standard Wiccan format, including casting a circle, invoking deities, and performing magical workings.

Harmony with Nature: Both Celtic spirituality and Wicca share a profound reverence for nature. Celtic Wiccans seek to harmonize their practices with the natural world, honoring the cycles of the moon, seasons, and the Earth itself.

Personalized Approach: Like Wicca, Celtic Wicca allows for a personalized and eclectic approach to spirituality. Practitioners often adapt rituals and practices to suit their individual preferences and needs.

Celtic Wicca offers a vibrant and spiritually fulfilling path for those drawn to the mystique of Celtic culture and the magic of Wicca. By merging these two traditions, practitioners find a unique way to connect with the divine, nature, and their own inner magic.

Eclectic Celtic Spirituality

Eclectic Celtic Spirituality is a diverse and adaptable path that allows individuals to craft a unique spiritual journey based on their personal preferences, experiences, and beliefs. Unlike more structured traditions like Druidry or Celtic Reconstructionism, eclectic Celtic spirituality has no rigid dogma or set rituals. Instead, it offers a framework that practitioners can modify and customize to suit their needs.

Blending Celtic Traditions

One of the defining characteristics of eclectic Celtic spirituality is its openness to blending Celtic traditions with other spiritual practices, philosophies, or belief systems. This syncretic approach enables practitioners to integrate elements from Celtic spirituality into their existing spiritual framework. For example, someone might incorporate Celtic deities into their Wiccan practice or combine Celtic rituals with mindfulness meditation.

Diversity Within Eclecticism

Eclectic Celtic spirituality is incredibly diverse due to the wide range of influences and practices it can incorporate. Here are some examples of how this diversity manifests:

Celtic Shamanism: Some practitioners may explore Celtic shamanic practices, connecting with the spirit world and embracing journeying, vision quests, or soul retrieval. This approach is often rooted in Celtic animism and a deep connection to the land.

Modern Witchcraft: Eclectic Celtic witches may draw from various forms of witchcraft, combining elements of spellwork, divination, and herbalism with Celtic deities and folklore. They might create their own unique rituals or adapt traditional ones to suit their needs.

Neo-Druidry with a Twist: Eclectic Druids may infuse their practice with elements from other earth-centered traditions or modern mindfulness techniques. They might incorporate practices like yoga, meditation, or energy work alongside Druidic rituals.

Interfaith Exploration: Some practitioners of eclectic Celtic spirituality explore connections between Celtic beliefs and other world religions, such as Buddhism or Hinduism. They seek common threads and shared wisdom to deepen their spiritual understanding.

Personal Growth and Exploration
Eclectic Celtic spirituality is a highly individualistic path that encourages personal growth and spiritual exploration. By crafting a unique blend of practices and beliefs, practitioners can tailor their spirituality to address their specific needs, questions, and aspirations. This freedom fosters a sense of empowerment and self-discovery.

The beauty of eclectic Celtic spirituality lies in its inclusivity, adaptability, and capacity to inspire a rich tapestry of personal connections with Celtic culture and spirituality. It's a living testament to the enduring relevance of Celtic wisdom in our ever-evolving world.

Celtic Spirituality in Everyday Life - A Deeper Exploration

For those who embrace Celtic spirituality, it is far more than a mere set of rituals or a periodic observance of festivals. It represents a profound philosophy that guides their daily existence. In this deeper exploration, we dissect the various facets of how Celtic spirituality becomes an intrinsic part of modern life.

Mindful Living and Sacred Moments
Celtic spirituality encourages living mindfully, savoring each moment as a gift from the natural world. Every sunrise, every rustle of leaves, and every encounter with a fellow being takes on a deeper significance. Practitioners often engage in daily rituals that serve as touchpoints of connection to this sacred

reality. Whether it's lighting a candle, reciting a blessing, or offering gratitude for the food on their table, these rituals are not performed out of habit but out of reverence.

The Tapestry of Nature

The Celtic understanding of nature is not as something separate but as an extension of the self. Daily life involves an intimate connection with the natural world. A walk in the forest is not just exercise but a spiritual journey, a conversation with the trees, and a communion with the spirits of the land. Practitioners might keep an altar adorned with items from the natural world - stones, feathers, or dried herbs - as a constant reminder of their interconnectedness with all life.

Creative Expression and Inspiration

Celtic spirituality serves as a wellspring of inspiration for artistic and creative pursuits. It finds expression not only in visual arts but also in literature, music, and poetry. Modern bards compose songs that echo with ancient melodies, and writers weave tales that draw upon Celtic myths and archetypes. Creativity, in turn, becomes a means of deepening one's spiritual connection and sharing it with others.

Community and Sharing

For many, Celtic spirituality is a communal experience. Practitioners gather in circles or groves to celebrate the seasons, share stories, and perform rituals together. These communities provide support, camaraderie, and a sense of belonging. It's not just about individual spiritual journeys but about creating a network of kindred spirits who walk the same path.

Ethical Living and Environmental Stewardship

Embedded within Celtic spirituality is a strong ethical foundation. Modern practitioners often extend their reverence for nature into active environmental stewardship. They participate in conservation efforts, reduce their ecological footprint, and promote sustainability. The Celtic concept of balance and harmony with the natural world guides their decisions, from what they eat to how they consume resources.

In this deeper exploration of Celtic spirituality in everyday life, we see how it isn't confined to a few practices or occasional moments of reverence. Instead, it is an all-encompassing way of being that imbues every aspect of life with meaning and purpose.

Simple Celtic Spirituality Practices

Celtic spirituality is known for its accessibility and inclusivity. Here are some simple practices that beginners can incorporate into their daily lives to start their journey on this spiritual path. These practices require no special tools or prior experience and can be adapted to suit individual preferences.

1. Morning Nature Connection
Begin your day with a moment of connection to nature. Find a quiet spot, whether it's your backyard, a nearby park, or even just gazing out of a window. Take a few deep breaths and observe the natural world around you. Listen to the birds, feel the breeze, or notice the sunlight filtering through the leaves. Express gratitude for this moment of communion with nature.

2. Mindful Walking
As you go about your daily walks or errands, practice mindful walking. Pay close attention to the sensation of each step - the pressure on your feet, the rhythm of your gait, and the ground beneath you. Imagine you are walking in harmony with the earth, feeling a profound connection with the land with every step you take.

3. Candle Meditation

Light a candle in a quiet, dimly lit space. Focus your attention on the flame. As you watch it flicker and dance, allow your mind to quiet and your thoughts to recede. This simple meditation can serve as a way to center yourself and find inner peace. You can also use this time for reflection or setting intentions for the day.

4. Daily Blessing

Before meals, take a moment to offer a simple blessing or expression of gratitude for the food you are about to eat. Acknowledge the journey of the ingredients from the earth to your plate. You can create your own blessing or use traditional ones, such as "Earth who gives to us this food, Sun who makes it ripe and good."

5. Elemental Awareness

Take time to connect with the four elements - Earth, Air, Fire, and Water. Spend a few minutes each day focusing on one element. For example, sit by a river or stream and contemplate the flow of water, or light a candle and meditate on the transformative power of fire. This practice helps you develop a deeper connection to the natural world.

6. Keep a Nature Journal

Carry a small notebook with you and jot down observations from your interactions with nature. Sketch the shapes of leaves, describe the colors of the sky, or write down the sounds you hear during a walk. Your journal becomes a personal record of your connection to the natural world.

7. Share a Story

Celtic spirituality has a rich tradition of storytelling. Share a meaningful story or myth with a friend or family member. Discuss its themes and what lessons or insights can be drawn from it. Storytelling can be a beautiful way to connect with others and explore the wisdom of Celtic traditions.

These beginner-friendly practices offer a taste of Celtic spirituality's deep connection to nature and the sacred. Feel free to adapt and modify them to suit your preferences and daily routine. As you continue your journey, you may choose to explore more advanced practices and rituals that resonate with you.

Conclusion: Nurturing the Flame of Celtic Wisdom

As we conclude our journey through the realms of Celtic mythology, spirituality, and culture, we find ourselves not at an end but rather at the beginning of a new chapter. The stories of the Celts, their deep reverence for the natural world, their enchanting myths, and their profound spiritual practices have left an indelible mark on our understanding of the human experience.

Celtic mythology, with its gods and goddesses, heroes and heroines, offers timeless lessons in courage, wisdom, and the eternal cycles of life, death, and rebirth. These stories continue to inspire and guide us, providing a wellspring of wisdom for navigating the complexities of our modern lives.

In exploring Celtic spirituality, we've uncovered the sacredness of the land, the significance of rituals, and the interconnectedness of all living things. The ancient Celts' profound respect for nature, their veneration of trees, rivers, and animals, serves as a poignant reminder of our own responsibility to protect and preserve the Earth.

Our journey has also taken us into the world of the Druids, the spiritual leaders and keepers of ancient wisdom. Their deep connection to nature, their role as intermediaries between worlds, and their unwavering commitment to the balance of the cosmos continue to inspire those who seek spiritual growth and enlightenment.

We've witnessed how Celtic culture has persisted through the ages, adapting and evolving, and how it continues to thrive in the hearts and minds of those who embrace it today. The resurgence of Celtic Paganism, Druidry, and related paths demonstrates the enduring power of these traditions in a modern context.

Our exploration of the Druidesses and the role of women in Celtic society revealed the remarkable contributions of female leaders, healers, and warriors. Their presence in Celtic culture challenges conventional notions of gender roles and highlights the importance of equality and inclusivity.

In the final chapter, we ventured into the living tradition of Celtic spirituality in the modern world. We encountered Neo-Paganism, Celtic Reconstructionism, Celtic Wicca, and Eclectic Celtic Spirituality, each offering a unique path for seekers to connect with the wisdom and traditions of the Celts.

As we conclude our journey, we are reminded that the wisdom of the Celts is not relegated to dusty history books but is very much alive in our hearts, our communities, and our connection to the natural world. The Celts, with their vibrant stories, their profound spirituality, and their enduring culture, invite us to carry the torch of their wisdom forward into the future.

In our own lives, we can draw upon the lessons of the Celts to cultivate a deeper connection with nature, a richer appreciation for the cycles of life, and a profound sense of spiritual wonder. Just as the Celts did, we can find inspiration and guidance in the beauty of the land around us, the stories that have been passed down through generations, and the wisdom of our own hearts.

May the flame of Celtic wisdom continue to burn brightly in your life, illuminating your path with its timeless brilliance.

And may you, like the Celts of old, find a deep and abiding connection to the natural world, to the spirits that dwell within it, and to the enduring magic of Celtic culture. Sláinte! (Cheers!)

Bibliography

Books:

Sjoestedt, Marie-Louise. "Celtic Gods and Heroes." Dover Publications, 2000.

MacCulloch, John Arnott. "The Religion of the Ancient Celts." CreateSpace Independent Publishing Platform, 2016.

Rolleston, Thomas. "Myths and Legends of the Celtic Race." CreateSpace Independent Publishing Platform, 2016.

Ellis, Peter Berresford. "The Druids." William B. Eerdmans Publishing Company, 1995.

Powell, T.G.E. "The Celts." Thames & Hudson, 1980.

Danaher, Kevin. "The Year in Ireland: Irish Calendar Customs." Mercier Press, 1972.

Davidson, Hilda Roderick Ellis. "Myths and Symbols in Pagan Europe: Early Scandinavian and Celtic Religions." Syracuse University Press, 1988.

MacCulloch, John Arnott. "Celtic Mythology." CreateSpace Independent Publishing Platform, 2015.

Rees, Alwyn, and Brinley Rees. "Celtic Heritage: Ancient Tradition in Ireland and Wales." Thames & Hudson, 1961.

Bonner, Mary. "The Cult of the Cat." Thames and Hudson, 1999.

Green, Miranda J. "The Gods of the Celts." Sutton Publishing, 2004.

MacCana, Proinsias. "Celtic Mythology." Peter Bedrick Books, 1983.

Condren, Mary. "The Serpent and the Goddess: Women, Religion, and Power in Celtic Ireland." HarperCollins, 1989.

Ellis, Peter Berresford. "A Dictionary of Irish Mythology." Oxford University Press, 1987.

Koch, John T. "Celtic Culture: A Historical Encyclopedia (Volumes 1-5)." ABC-CLIO, 2006.

MacKillop, James. "Dictionary of Celtic Mythology." Oxford University Press, 1998

Markale, Jean. "The Celts: The People Who Came out of the Darkness." Inner Traditions, 1999.

Matthews, John. "The Druid Source Book: From Earliest Times to the Present Day." Blandford Press, 1996.

Websites:

"Celtic Mythology." Ancient History Encyclopedia. https://www.ancient.eu/Celtic_Mythology/

"Celtic Religion." Encyclopedia Britannica. https://www.britannica.com/topic/Celtic-religion

"Celtic Gods and Goddesses." The Celtic Literature Collective. http://www.maryjones.us/ctexts/gods.html

"The Celtic Pantheon: Gods and Goddesses." Mythology.net. https://mythology.net/celtic/celtic-pantheon/

"The Celts: History, Life, and Culture." National Geographic. https://www.nationalgeographic.com/history/magazine/2018/03-04/celts-a-history/

"Celtic Mythology." The New World Encyclopedia. https://www.newworldencyclopedia.org/entry/Celtic_mythology

Academic Papers:

Lincoln, Bruce. "The Indo-European Myth of Creation." History of Religions, Vol. 21, No. 4 (May, 1982), pp. 289-302.

Littleton, C. Scott. "The Bull-Roarer in Celtic Religion." History of Religions, Vol. 7, No. 4 (May, 1968), pp. 370-389.

Ross, Anne. "The Early Germans." History Today, Vol. 30, No. 4 (Apr, 1980), pp. 23-30.

Made in the USA
Las Vegas, NV
27 June 2024

91549010R00079